St. Mary of the Angels, Worthing

The Gaisford family and

Our Lady of Sion Convent.

150 Years

Of

Entwined History.

Dennis J Key

ACKNOWLEDGEMENTS

A book of this type is very dependent on the help of others, and I express my thanks to all those who assisted me in various ways.

To Mrs. Toni Dowd, now of Rustington parish, who ensured that many papers once stored in the basement of the presbytery in Gratwicke Road were copied and the originals sent, for safe-keeping to Bishop's House, Hove. Toni compiled a file of these copies held by the Parish Priest together with a collection of photographs. These include both historical and present church views together with details of many of the religious church items that are mentioned in the body of this history.

To Julian St. Lawrence of Howth Castle, Dublin. It is hard to express fully my thanks for his help in providing the photographs of Thomas and Lady Emily Gaisford. His correction of my errors in Gaisford history were a distinct help in making the early story so much more accurate.

To Sister Carolyn and the Sisters of Sion for information about the early days of the Convent.

To the Archivist of the Archdiocese of Southwark, Jenny Delves, and to Hazel State, Archivist of the Diocese of Arundel and Brighton, for their valuable help and patience.

To the staff of Worthing Library for guidance and help searching so successfully through the records held in the Reference Library.

To present and former Parishioners of St. Mary's for providing photographs, booklets and most important of all memories of former times and events that were so important to examine and hear about. Without that help, much would be lost forever, never to be documented on paper. I have not been able to list all these people. With great respect to other un-named people, I would like to pick out Michael and Ros (nee Whibley) Burholt, Brendan and Marguerite Gudule (nee Mottram) Balhetchet for information and lastly Bert and Violet (nee Flynn) Kent. To Anne Topping for translations and Norma (nee Topping) Ndoping and Bryan Robinson both for proof-reading. Their help was greatly appreciated and I thank each of them sincerely. All documents and photographs offered to me for use in this book have been either stored in the parish archive filing or returned to their owners.

To Bill and Mae Day for memories and booklets of the early days of the pre-parish St. Michael's church community at High Salvington.

To Bernard and Norma Markham of English Martyrs for providing a copy of a letter from Canon Westlake which was very pertinent.

To John and Angela Finch of St. Charles for information of the creation of St. Charles Borromeo Parish in East Worthing.

To Alan Stepney of St. Mary's for his guidance in all things electronic and graphical.

To Trevor Stauss of Storrington parish for technical knowledge.

To Rebecca Paynter for her photographic skills and productions.

To all who assisted in bringing this book from first draft to the final published copy produced so successfully by Chris Powell and his staff at Verite CM. Sincere thanks for your help, Chris.

And finally, to my wife Jacqueline, for her patience when I so often told her – and bored her greatly - of the 'latest snippet I've found'.

Information is now in the public domain on Historical Web pages, the National Archives at Kew, the National Newspaper Records at Colindale, Genealogy Sites, Worthing Library and Wikipedia.

For information on the Gaisford family, I have used all these sources extensively together with the records of the local paper, the Worthing Herald, held by Worthing Reference Library.

I have also referred to the following:-

Colin Clark & Rupert Taylor. 'Worthing at War', (1989).

D. Robert Elleray. A.L.A., F.R.S.A. 'The Roman Catholics in Worthing', (1987).

W. T. Pike, ed., 'Sussex in the Twentieth Century', (1910).

Henfry Smail. 'Notable People of Sussex', (1950).

Diocese of Arundel and Brighton monthly paper, the 'A & B News'.

If there are any errors, factual or otherwise, they are mine and I apologise for them. I was so aware that names in some places on those early handwritten pages of the Memoranda by Rev. Father Whiteside and the Journal of Rev. Father Purdon were difficult to decipher but I believe fair interpretations have been made.

Dennis Key,
Worthing.
May 11 2015

CONTENTS

Acknowledgements
List of Illustrations
Appendix

LIST OF ILLUSTRATIONS

APPENDIX - CLERGY WHO HAVE SERVED AT ST. MARY'S, WORTHING

PARISH PRIESTS		CURATES	
SOUTHWARK DIOCESE			
Rev. Wollett	1859		
Rev. Riordan	1859		
Rev. J. MacDonald	1860		
Rev. M. J. Fannan	1861 - 64		
Rev. Richard Schofield	1863 - 64		
Rev. J. MacDonald	1864 - 65		
Rev. Henry Whiteside	1865 - 70		
Rev. Canon J. Purdon	1870 - 23	John Fichter	1908 – 18
Rev. Canon C. M. Westlake		E.J. Redding	1918 – 22
1923 – 58 (died in office)		James Walters	1922 – 24
		Francis Dorman	1924 – 25
		Cecil H. Tasker	1925 – 29
		Thomas Byrne	1927 – 28
		Maurice Byron	1927 – 28
		Andrew Shaw	1928 – 30
		Hopetoun Currie	1930 – 34
		James Barraud	1930 – 39
		Andrew Convey	1934 – 42
		Joseph Sulliway	1938 – 40
		Dennis Cullen	1940 – 43
		Donald Wilkins	1940 – 47
		Cyril Hanrahan	1942 – 43
		Michael Dunning	1943 – 54
		Philip Wroe	1945 – 47
		Edm. Arbuthnott	1947 – 48
		Gerald O'Sullivan	1947 – 57

PARISH PRIESTS		CURATES	
SOUTHWARK DIOCESE			
		Richard Veal	1956 – 67
		Francis Davys	1957 – 58
		Jerem. Corcaran	1957 – 66
Rev. Mgr. Denis Wall	1958–66	Brian O'Sullivan	1958 – 62
d. October 1992		Matt. McInerney	1963 – 76
ARUNDEL & BRIGHTON DIOCESE			
Rev. Mgr. Arthur Iggleden	1966–81	William Dunne	1966 – 71
d. June 2001		Patrick Olivier	1967 – 72
		John Nuttall	1972 – 77
		David Foley	1972 – 80
		W. Oliver Heaney	1975 – 78
		Michael Jackson	1977 – 79
		M. Thompson	1979 – 81
		James Maguire	1980 – 81
Rev. Anthony Shelley	1981 – 90	Paul Sankey	1982 – 84
Ret.		Michael Walsh	1982 – 86
		R. Madders	1984 – 85
		D. Sutcliffe	1986 – 89
		D. Russell	1987 – 88
		P. Turner	1989 – 93
Rev. Canon Tony Clarke	1990 – 04	A. Milner	1993 – 96
d. April 2007		G. Thompson	1996 – 00
		P. Wilkinson	2000 – 04
Revs. Gardiner & Kelly	2004 – 2007		
Rev. Chris Benyon	2007 – to date		

DEACONS   Kenneth Leach 1976 – 80   Colin Wolczak 1986 – 87
              Robert Mason   1996 – 04

CHAPTER 1

Worthing – a place to visit

In the mid-18th century, Brighton was described by Richard Russell, a local doctor, as an ideal venue to receive what he referred to as his 'sea-water' cure. This was the bathing in and drinking of sea-water.

The town was visited regularly by members of the British Royal Family and this inevitably led to rich, upper class members of society wanting to experience the pleasures of seaside visits themselves. With easy access from the capital, Brighton grew in popularity and success.

Just 10 miles or so along the coast was a small unimportant fishing village surrounded by farmland. Worthing was linked by road to Brighton in the east and to Broadwater in the north, an ancient manor dating back many years. Because of its more sheltered location, nestling at the foot of the South Downs, its climate was much better than its bigger and well-known coastal neighbour.

Princess Amelia, born in 1783, was the youngest daughter of King George III and his Queen Consort Charlotte. She generally suffered from fragile health and developed severe pain in her knee in 1798. Her doctors advised 'the sea-water' cure and looked for a location other than the busy and prosperous Brighton. They decided that Worthing was a very suitable venue for improving her health and pains. She ultimately spent five months in the village and, as a result, Worthing became known to society and grew from a village to a small town. The local authorities took the initiative to make the growing town a high-class seaside resort and spa adding attractions to encourage 'fashionable' people to stay. In 1807 there were over 2000 living in the town that by then had new amenities ranging from a chapel to a theatre.

Before 1778 when the First Relief Act, commonly called 'The Papists Act', was passed, the members of the Roman Catholic community were not ensured full rights of citizenship within the United Kingdom.

The Act changed this and also repealed the law that allowed the Catholic Mass only to be celebrated in certain registered private chapels. With no private chapels owned by Catholics in Worthing, the nearest services would have been celebrated in either Brighton or Arundel.

CHAPTER 2

A Gaisford beginning

It would do an injustice to the Gaisford family not to give the background story to the connection which that family had to the church of St. Mary of the Angels. Without the tremendous support of one member of this family in particular, this story may well have been so different. Thomas Gaisford, and his wife Lady Emily, gave considerable support in effort and money to provide the fledgling Catholic Community in Worthing the church they so needed and desired.

The Very Rev. Thomas Gaisford, D.D., M.A., was born at Iford Manor of very minor landed gentry in 1779 and inherited the estate in 1810 on the death of his father.

Very Rev. T. Gaisford D.D.

By 1812 he was Regius Professor of Greek at Oxford University. He was ordained to the Anglican priesthood in 1815.

On July 11 1815 he married Helen Margaret, the daughter of a fellow Anglican priest, Rev. Robert Douglas. With Margaret, Thomas had two sons, Thomas, born on December 12 1816, and William.

The birth of the elder son had an immense effect on the later Catholic population in the seaside town of Worthing in the county of Sussex.

In 1829 when offered the position of Bishop of Oxford, he declined it.

On March 8 1830, Helen, his wife of fifteen years, died.

In 1831 Thomas became the well known and respected Dean Thomas Gaisford of Christ Church, Oxford a position he held until his death.

Dean Thomas then married again. Once more he chose the daughter of an Anglican priest, his second wife, Jane Catharine, being the daughter of the Rev. John Jenkins and sister of the Very Rev. R. Jenkins DD, Master of Balliol. There was no issue of this marriage.

On June 23 1843 his 21 year old son William encountered difficulties while swimming in the River Thames near Oxford. His friend Richard Phillimore entered the water to save him but both tragically drowned.

Dean Thomas died on June 2 1855 and Thomas inherited Iford Manor.Two years later he made a life-changing decision.

Meanwhile, a baby girl had been born on December 18 1829. Her name was Lady Emily St. Lawrence. Her father was Sir Thomas St. Lawrence 3rd Earl of Howth (near Dublin), who was a member of the Church of Ireland. Her mother was Lady Emily de Burgh who was the daughter of the 13th Earl of Clanricarde and a Catholic. She was brought up in her mother's faith while her brother was brought up in the father's faith as was the custom at that time.

Although her mother died in December 1842 just two weeks before Lady Emily's 13th birthday, she retained her Catholic faith.

From press reports of that time, she lived a very full social life. Being the eldest daughter of the Earl of Howth it fell on her to escort her father to the many society gatherings of that time.

It is recorded that on January 12 1847, aged 17 she was at a dinner party with several similarly entitled people at the home of the Lord Lieutenant of Ireland. This appears to be a bi-annual event. She attended Lady Palmerston's 1st Ball of the Season on Friday 02 June 1848.

Thomas Gaisford, junior, was a very respectable person, confirmed by descriptions of the gentleman to be read on later pages in this history. He must have been known to this attractive young lady, from within an international circle, through interactions with family connections in both countries. He was pursuing a career in the Army and had achieved the rank of Captain in the year that Emily is first recorded in the Society columns of the press.

CHAPTER 3

Thomas Gaisford and his family

From the number of articles seen on Wikipedia, Dean Thomas Gaisford, was a well known, almost national figure. The brief details included in the previous chapter do not give him justice.

For simplicity, Thomas junior, is hereafter referred to as Thomas. He joined the Army and was 'gazetted' Captain on May 28 1847 with the Hungerford Troop of Yeomanry Cavalry, also known as the 79th Foot and Wiltshire Militia. These units were formed in 1820 for Military Service in aid of the Civil Power in absence of organised police forces.

A description of the man was given many years later by the reporter of the Worthing Gazette. He wrote of a man 'of excellent figure, handsome features and soldierly appearance .... A man of culture, a linguist and a connoisseur... He was educated at Rugby and at Christ Church. He was a member of the Roxburghe Club.' The Roxburghe Club was/is an exclusive bibliophilic and publishing society with the number of members at any one time limited to forty. He was a member from 1858 until his death in 1898.

He married his first wife on January 31 1850 at Lacock Abbey, near Chippenham, Wiltshire. She was Horatia Maria Fielding, the daughter of Rear Admiral Charles and Lady Elizabeth Fielding.

Her sister was a lady in waiting to Queen Victoria and she was a half sister to William Henry Fox-Talbot a British inventor and photography pioneer. He invented the calotype (or talbotype) process of photography, a precursor to photographic processes of the later 19th and 20th centuries. The photograph shown below is believed to be one of the first photographs of this type.

They had a son, Horace Charles born on July 26 1851 in Belgrave Square, London, and baptised on August 11 by the Rev. George Gaisford in St. Peter's Church, Pimlico, London. It was reported that Horatia died in 1851 soon after the birth. It was claimed by Agatha, one of the daughters of Thomas by his second wife Lady Emily, in later years, that Horatia sent for a priest on her death bed but this was refused by her husband, Thomas. Whether this story is true or apocryphal is unproven.

Thomas Gaisford and Horatia Fielding c. 1850

Thomas would have had good reason not to convert to the Catholic faith while his father was alive. Six years after the death of Horatia, Thomas was received into the Church with his son Horace by Cardinal Henry Edward Manning. Cardinal Manning was himself received into the Church as a convert clergyman in 1851 and was created a Cardinal in 1875.

In the report, mentioned above, in the Worthing Gazette it stated that, in March 1862 Thomas succeeded as commanding officer of the 1st Administrative Battalion of the Berkshire Regiment of Yeoman Cavalry (Hungerford), a position with the rank of Major, which he held until June 1872.

It is the belief of the Gaisford family that Wiltshire was a particularly unwelcoming county to Catholics. The Gaisfords were much married into the Anglican clergy and had many friends who were clergymen. Thomas may have felt no longer acceptable at Iford Manor and looked for a home in a place more hospitable. Some seven years after the death of Horatia, Thomas may also have been drawn to Worthing, with its proximity to the Duke of Norfolk's seat at Arundel.

In 1858 he heard that a Mr. James Basil Daubuz, appointed the High Sheriff of Sussex in 1845, wanted to sell his home, Offington Hall, with the surrounding estate in Worthing, Sussex. The property was ideal for a man who was planning to marry soon. The house and 121 acres cost Thomas £11,400. The sale was completed and extensive alterations and additions including a chapel, all costing a further £5,000 were undertaken. Before the chapel was completed the family believe that the end of the drawing room was used for 'church services'.

The London Daily News of October 3 1859 informed its readers that 'The Lady Emily St. Lawrence is about to bestow her hand upon Mr. T. Gaisford.'

On November 8 1859 The Sussex Advertiser duly reported the following marriage having taken place,

'1859, 26 October, marriage of Thomas and Lady Emily. Celebrated in the village of Howth in Ireland. Thomas Gaisford has lately purchased the beautiful domain of Offington, near Worthing, for a permanent residence. Amongst those present were, Lord St. Lawrence, brother of the bride, Colonel Gaisford, brother of the bridegroom.'

It was reported that Thomas was 'one of the earliest converts of the Tractarian movement, the trusted friend of Newman and Manning, and a pillar of the Roman Catholic Church in the South of England'. In a letter from a Fr. Ratisbonne dated 1862 to the convent authorities in France, he is referred to as 'one of the converts to Catholicism.'

The Gaisfords also had a home at 12 Bruton Street, Mayfair, London.

The London Standard of October 1 1860 reported thus,

'1860, 25 September, a son, Cyril St. Lawrence born .... at Brighton.'

Eighteen months later the Newcastle Journal, of April 3 1862 reported,

'1862, 28 March, a son, Julian Charles, born .... at Offington, Sussex.'

Julian Charles will be seen again later in this work and his descendant, also Julian, was instrumental in having pictures of the parents of these children included in the Colour Plates section of this book.

Against the pleasure of a growing family, there was also sadness.

On September 28 1862, the death of Cyril St. Lawrence Gaisford occurred in Worthing, days after his second birthday.

But life for the Gaisfords continued as the Morning Post of September 9 1863 informed its readers,

'1863, 5 September, a daughter, Teresa Mary, born at Offington.'

The Belfast News-Letter of August 25 1865 reported a birth,

6

'1865, 20 August, a daughter Mary Emily, at 12 Bruton St., London.' Mary later married Mr. George McKelder.

On September 28 1866, the Dublin Evening Mail described a birth,

'1866, 24 September, a daughter Agatha Mary, at Bruton St., London.' Agatha lived unmarried and died in London in 1953.

One of the boys had been unwell enough to need certain care for in a letter to Thomas, dated July 24 1867, Bishop Grant wrote,

'I hope your boy has returned full of health and vigour from Edgbaston and has found you and your lady and his little sister well.'

On November 16 1867, the Sussex Agricultural Express wrote,

'1867, 6 October, a daughter .... born at Offington House.'

And finally on November 9 1868, the Pall Mall Gazette reported thus,

'1868, 31 October, a son, Basil St. Lawrence, at Offington, Sussex, born to Lady Emily Gaisford'.

Basil became a clergyman and died in 1914.

(It is interesting to note that The Morning Post of June 6 1898 included a report referring to recently deceased Thomas Gaisfords Will and bequests. A Codicil to his Will dated May 26 1897 referred to two sons, Julian and the Rev. Basil, and three daughters Mary Teresa, Mary Emily and Agatha Mary. The daughter reported to have been born at Offington in October 1867 is not included but no reference to a death of a female Gaisford child with or without name has been found in the National Records.)

Nine years after his marriage, Thomas was dealt a terrible blow when his dear wife unexpectedly died, possibly after childbirth, aged just 39 years on November 6 1868. Their eldest child, Julian Charles, six weeks before, had celebrated his eighth birthday and their last child had been born just one week before. It must have been a devastating time for him.

In The Morning Post of November 9 1868 we are told that,

'We have to report the death of Lady Emily Gaisford ...... at Offington.'

Lady Emily was interred in the vault inside the church of St. Mary of the Angels by Bishop Grant on November 11 with an infant child. (This may have been the unregistered infant daughter who may have been a foetal death, incorrectly reported by the Sussex Agricultural Express, in November 1867).

The vault was included in the design of the church but few would have believed that it would be needed just four years later.

That visit to Worthing and the church he nurtured was the Bishops last, as he died in Rome on May 31 1870 having suffered with cancer for some time.

On June 20 1870, Thomas married for a third time and his children once more had a mother to care for them. Their new stepmother was Lady Alice Mary Kerr, (b. 1837). She was the only child of the seventh Marquis of Lothian. She was a noted photographer who had a specific and unusual approach to portraiture for that time.

In the mid 19th century portraiture was seen as one of the central functions of photography. At the same time as the production of this history, The British Library is currently (2015) exhibiting highlights from its vast collection of early photography. Of that period they state that 'some of the best work was, in fact, being produced by amateurs, among them Lady Alice Mary Kerr. Only a few examples of her work survive but her portrait studies .... are particularly powerful.' There is work by William Henry Fox Talbot included in this exhibition.

The family welcomed a half-brother to the family when in 1871 Walter Thomas was born in Sussex. He is referred to later in this account as a casualty of the First World War.

Hugh William, a son was born in Bruton Street on August 13 1874. He married Virginia Bryce on May 11 1904 and was Consul General in Munich, 1925 – 32.

On October 27 1876 the last child of Thomas, named Bernard Henry, was born in Bruton Street but he died two months later.

It was later reported in the Kent and Sussex Courier in September 1879 that the eldest son of Thomas, Horace Charles, serving in the Grenadier Guards had died, in the Registration District of East Preston.

In spite of the recorded births, the marriage was not a success and by 1880 they were living separate lives. Lady Alice died in Killarney on January 25 1892 aged 55 years and was buried there. This explains why no record of burial or grave can be found in Worthing papers of Lady Alice Gaisford.

CHAPTER 4

The Mission Territory of Britain

From 1688 English Catholics were governed from Rome as a missionary territory through Vicars Apostolic who were directly responsible to the Sacred Congregation for the Propagation of the Faith in the Vatican. There were four such vicars having 'Districts' - these being London, Midland, Northern and Western.

Before 1829, when the final Catholic Relief Act was passed by Parliament, Roman Catholics were not allowed to hold public office and suffered from legal and social disabilities. Since Elizabethan times, officially, the Penal laws disallowed the Mass to be said but gradually a blind eye was given to this practice. There were still members of old aristocratic and upper class families who had kept the Faith secretly or quietly and had large houses with chapels included in their designs. Under the Penal Laws if the owners desired, those chapels could be registered for celebration of the Mass in private. As a result Mass was celebrated in those houses with the local Catholic community invited to be present.

Small groups of Catholics in any location were described as attending a 'Mission' these groups being served by travelling priests. If there was a nearby mansion with a resident priest, he was also invited to celebrate Mass for the local community on Sundays.

In 1840 four new vicariates were formed, the London District was divided into Westminster and Southwark, Midland District was divided with the Central District being formed, Northern District had Lancashire added and the Western District had the new Welsh District added.

At this time from the 1830's there appeared what is termed 'the Oxford Movement' when many Anglicans joined together as Anglo-Catholics or took the great leap to join the rapidly blossoming Church of Rome. Fr. John Henry Newman from Oxford, once more connected to this History, may be the most well known and is now Blessed John Henry Newman.

In 1850 a Roman Catholic hierarchy was re-established with Cardinal Wiseman arriving in September as the first Archbishop of Westminster. Twelve bishops were given territorial dioceses under the Cardinal Archbishop. One of these Bishoprics was that of Southwark, south of the river Thames and including Surrey, Sussex, Hampshire, Berkshire, the Isle of Wight and the Channel Islands.

CHAPTER 5

Southwark Diocese and Worthing before 1861

On June 27 1851 Dr. Thomas Grant was appointed Bishop of Southwark and was consecrated on July 6 in Rome by Cardinal Franzoni. He had been ordained on November 28 1841 in Rome and was appointed the rector of the English College there at the early age of 44. He guided his newly formed diocese for nineteen years, agreeing to the formation of many Missions, as Parishes were called in those days, including Worthing, and died in Rome while attending the Vatican Council in 1870.

When he died, the Bishop of Birmingham, the Most Rev. William Bernard Ullathorne, O.S.B., wrote of him 'He was a brilliant student with a prodigious memory and a fine linguist fluent in Latin, French and Italian. ..... He was a child of prayer and a slave of duty and charity. Many of his contemporaries considered him a Saint ....'. Southwark was so fortunate to be blessed with a Bishop considered one of the greatest in nineteenth century Catholic circles.

The Gaisfords had organised a Chaplain to celebrate Mass in their new chapel in Offington Hall. They agreed to allow the small local Catholic community to attend Mass at their home. For the more wealthy residents of Worthing and those Catholics visiting Worthing, travel out to Offington would have been by horse drawn coach. The journey to the estate and subsequent travel from gatehouse to Hall would have caused little inconvenience. Those not so lucky had a tiring journey of a long walk to and from the Gaisford home.

In 1859 Count de Torre Diaz and a few other Catholics petitioned the Bishop to open a Mission in Worthing ministered by the Rev. Wollett, chaplain to Offington Hall, and a Mission Church was opened using the chapel in his home, Augusta House, in Augusta Place, named after the elder sister of Princess Amelia, in August of that year. The house was originally named Trafalgar House and was later called Stanhoe Hall. It finally became the Stanhoe Hotel. It is also believed that in 1859 a Rev. Riordon took over the Chaplaincy, but this cannot be verified.

Fr. Purdon, a future parish priest of St. Mary's confirmed this in an interview included in the June 2 1900 edition of the Worthing Intelligencer. He listed many members of the European Catholic nobility who visited Worthing at that earlier time.

The Mission needed a formal home near the town centre and Bishop Grant was very keen to develop the Mission in Worthing. His aim was to provide a resident priest with a formal church building for worship.

To this end he looked to another Catholic institution for co-operation. He approached the Sisters of Our Lady of Sion with a proposition which was agreed.

And so the interaction of parish church and convent with school began and this has lasted for more than 150 years. Today when premises larger than the church Social Area are required for an important function, Headmaster Mr. Michael Scullion so often agrees to the church using the comparatively enormous school hall.

It is probable that at this time Thomas Gaisford was troubled by his treatment of his first wife Horatia when she was dying. It may be recalled that he would not allow a priest to be with her. It might be believed that it was for this reason that he contributed so generously to the building of the new church in Worthing.

Dr Thomas Grant - Bishop of Southwark

CHAPTER 6

Offington

As is mentioned earlier, on October 26 1859, the marriage of Thomas and Lady Emily St. Lawrence was celebrated in the village of Howth in Ireland.

The Gaisford family moved into Offington soon after the marriage.

It had a Chapel with sitting room for 25 and the Catholic faithful were allowed to attend Mass at Offington from November 1859. By this time the resident Chaplain is believed to be Fr. Collingridge who dedicated the altar there to St. Thomas of Canterbury.

The use of Stanhoe Hall could not have been very successful. Soon after, in September, the portable altar and vestments were taken to Offington Hall where the new chapel was now used for Mass.

Nothing more is heard of the previously mentioned Rev. Wollett but between 1859 and 1860 two priests are mentioned, Fr. Ignatius Collingridge and Fr. Eugene Riordon.

Of Fr. Collingridge we can read two items from local papers of the time,

The Newcastle Courant, April 16 1852 stated,

'The churchwardens of the parish of St. Thomas, Winchester, distrained (*i.e. claimed ownership*) a few days ago, on the goods of the Rev. I. Collingridge, Roman Catholic priest, in consequence of the non-payment of two church rates, amounting to twenty-five shillings.'

The Salisbury and Winchester Journal on April 6 1867 informed that,

'The Visiting Justices will present their report upon the application of the Rev. I. Collingridge to be allowed to celebrate Divine services with the Roman Catholic prisoners (*in Winchester gaol*) with greater facilities than at present.'

Of Fr. Reardon (*Riordon*) we can read just one item in the Salisbury & Winchester Journal of April 20 1861 it was recorded that,

'Fr. Reardon (*sic*) was formerly Chaplain to Sir James Doughty Tichbourne of Alresford, Hants. His son (Sir James) married the Hon. Teresa Mary, eldest daughter of Lord and Lady Arundell'.

One may assume that Major Thomas and Lady Emily heard of Fr. Riordon through social connections with the landed gentry of the time as a castle mentioned is near the home of the Wiltshire Gaisfords.

According to records held by the Convent of Sion, for a short time the intention was to name the Mission after St. Symphorian but this may have been dropped when it was found that there was already an Anglican church of St. Symphorian in Durrington, a village just outside the town to the North West. During 1864 it was officially named Our Lady of the Angels but was finally dedicated to St Mary of the Angels.

From February 10 1864 until 1867, Fr. J. McDonald served as chaplain at Offington Hall. Little information could be found of this priest but in a letter of July 24 1867 the Bishop advised Thomas Gaisford that, "due to Fr. McDonald's years and standing" he had appointed Fr. Fannan to serve the people of Worthing as priest and to be his Chaplain.

Offington Hall with wing and chapel added in 1858

CHAPTER 7

The Sisters of Our Lady of Sion and St. Mary's Worthing

The Ratisbonne family were Jewish merchants in Strasbourg, France.

Two of the sons, Rev. Frs. Maria Theodor and Marie - Alphonse, converted and became Catholic priests. The main aim of the convert brothers was the promotion of true understanding between Jews and Christians and to use education as a means to this end.

The brothers founded an Order of Religious in Paris. They called the order 'The Congregation of Religious (Sisters) of Our Lady of Sion'. The brother priests were very interested in expanding the Order into other countries but an attempt in 1858 to found a House in England, at Greenwich, was unsuccessful. Bishop Grant, aware of this failure, contacted the Order on the possibilities of them being interested in a joint venture of building both a convent and church connected on adjoining sites in Worthing.

Fr. Theodore wrote several letters to persons unknown. In early 1862 he wrote, and a modern translation, obtained with the help of parishioner Anne, reads,

"Near this town (Worthing), called "the English Nice" because of its mild climate, the highly respected Major Gaisford, one of the converts to Catholicism, was residing in Offington Hall. This gentleman had conceived the idea of building, in entirely protestant Worthing, a church corresponding to the needs of Catholics drawn there by the attraction of the beach. With the co-operation of a teaching Order, the Bishop (Grant) was hoping to make this church the centre of a flourishing mission. The providential establishment of the Worthing Foundation is such that we can perceive many fruitful blessings in it".

Thomas Gaisford found a suitable site and conferred with Bishop Grant about the purchase of land for the site of the Mission church and Convent. The Order of Our Lady of Sion agreed to the proposals put forward by the Diocese. There was the matter to be considered about the accommodation of the Sisters before they could take possession of their new convent buildings. Temporary premises were needed and the problem was solved when a building in North Street was found to be for sale. Some ten years before, Wortley House had been the Wortley House Academy. It was located in North Street on a site where the north east corner of the current Lidl store is situated.

The property was purchased in November 1862 and made suitable for the Sisters of the Order. A Chapel was created in this building capable of holding about 14 people and from November 9 Mass was offered there using the altar and vestments passed over from Offington Hall.

The Catholic community in Worthing then moved their place of worship from the chapel in Offington Hall to the chapel in Wortley House.

The premises were dedicated to St. Teresa of Avila and this name was transferred to the Convent on occupation. The name still lives on to this day. The development built in 1975 by the Order on former convent ground in Gratwicke Road is named Avila House.

On November 4 1862 Fr. Theodore wrote, again to persons unknown and again translated through Anne reads,

"Worthing is a delightful place by the sea very near Brighton, two and a half hours from London by train. The upper classes go there in crowds. Catholics have neither a church nor spiritual help, so they are very anxious to have our foundation. We have rented a large house, suitable for a boarding-school, and at the same time, we have bought a large wooded beautiful property where we shall later build our convent".

A further letter dated December 25 1862 from Fr. Theodore to persons unknown, once more, is translated thus,

"The Worthing Foundation gives me so much consolation and joy! This little establishment will grow and bear fruit: I hope that the construction plans contain provision for a substantial annex for the Catechumenate. There must be a worthy shelter for Protestant and Israelite girls. However, in order for this shelter to have adequate resources without recourse to special collections and charitable donations, it must be under the same roof as a fine boarding school. Unless we have dividends from shares to support this charitable work, it is prudent and it is necessary to humbly create other financial resources and I see nothing worthier and more beneficial than resources provided by a boarding school".

The move into the newly completed convent took place in the latter part of September 1864 with three sisters taking up residence. In earlier days, religious Sisters took the title 'Mother', so Mother Louise Weywada led Mother Desiree and Mother Nazarena Autori into their new home.

CHAPTER 8

St. Mary of the Angels 1861 – 1870

Catholic families either living in or visiting Worthing who wished to fulfil their obligation to hear Mass on Sunday undertook a long journey. They either travelled to Brighton on the one side or Arundel on the other. The Chapel of Offington being in the interior of the house, at some distance from Worthing, and far from the public road, did not satisfy the wish that had been expressed for a Catholic Church in the town.

Meanwhile in Autumn 1861 Fr. Michael J. Fannan arrived in Worthing to be in charge of the Mission and the Chaplaincy. He would have found himself immediately involved in discussions about developments with Thomas Gaisford, the Sisters of Sion and Bishop Grant.

The following information is taken from various items of correspondence in the Archive file.

A list of 'Subscriptions for purchasing the site and building a permanent Chapel at Worthing' was noted in February 1862.

Those giving more than £5 were,

Mr. Gaisford of Offington gave £1000, Rev. Ignatius Collingbridge £115, Mr. Hope Scott £100, Lady Emily Gaisford £50, Charles Gould gave £25 and the Duke of Norfolk, Henry Munster and N. Power gave £10 each.

Three people gave five guineas. They were Mr. Blunt, Mr. & Mrs. Callaghan and W. H. Roe.

Donations of £5 were given by :-

A Friend in Worthing, A Well Wisher, Henry Barnswall, Rev. M. Fannan, Miss Idsher (?), C. Lampays, Lady McFarlane, P. O'Connor, Mr. E. Wheble, De Zulueta and J. S. Z. (Zulueta?).

The donations totalled £1447 and four shillings.

All parties agreed to the purchase of a plot of freehold land covering an area stretching south of Richmond Road between Crescent Road on the East and Gratwicke Road on the West. The price was £248 and ten shillings and the site was bought in October 1862 from Messrs. Hide and Patching by the Bishop of Southwark and other Trustees.

On April 14 1863, the conveyance of the land was completed. Henry Clutton of 9, The Burlington, London and an expert in French medieval architecture, was asked to draw up a design for a combined church and convent. He chose the use of red brick, Bath and Pulborough stone and flint. The design allowed for the easy future extension when required. The contract to build 'a part of a New Catholic Church in the said Town of Worthing' was given to the local firm of Blaker and signed in the presence of the Bishop. Thomas Gaisford undertook to pay the sum of £1081 being 80% of the expected costs. The residual money of 20% would be paid three months after completion and delivery of the building. Bishop Grant laid the foundation stone of Our Lady of the Angels on May 4 1863. The ceremony was witnessed by a large crowd, Catholic and non-Catholic.

On February 10 1864, Fr. Fannan left the Mission. Two days before he left he produced a document listing monies expended to Feb. 8 1864.

'To Mr. Clutton for drawings etc for the original Church as proposed at Chapel house	£ 8. 10. 0
Purchase of Site from Messrs. Hide & Patching	£248. 10. 0
Mr. Edmunds for Conveyancing	£ 27. 5. 7
Mr. Blaker on account	£250. 0. 0
Ditto	£250. 0. 0
Ditto	£400. 0. 0
Small sums expended by Rev. M. Fannan for cards etc.	£ 1. 0. 1
Total	£1185. 5. 8.

A meeting was held that day, present Rev. R. Schofield, Rev. M. Fannan, Mr. Gaisford – the accounts of subscriptions for the Catholic Church at Worthing were produced by the Rev. M. Fannan. The result is as follows, viz.

Money received up to this date (as above)	£1185. 5. 8
In Mr. Gaisford's hands	£ 147. 9. 7
Ditto	£ 114. 4. 5
Total	£ 261. 14. 0

The Rev. M. Fannan handed over to Mr. Gaisford the balance of monies rec'd by him.

Signed   Gaisford (*sic*), M. Fannan and Richard Schofield

There is a complication found here as a 'Memoranda' written by Fr. Whiteside states that "The Rev. Fr. Richard Schofield had charge of the Mission from May 1863 to November 1864". The Memoranda can be found below.

Fr. Schofield had been received into the Catholic Church from the Anglican Church by Fr. Newman in 1850.

It then followed that the Bishop referred, in a letter to Major Gaisford, to his writing to Fr. Schofield about the accounts (*of the building costs of the new church?*). In this letter he writes 'I fully adopt and confirm the title of Our Lady of the Angels' as the name of the church. (*The original title should be noted.*)

A letter to Thomas Gaisford from Bishop Grant, dated March 25 1864

With one word indecipherable, the transcription reads thus,

'

St. George's

March 25th 1864

Dear Major Gaisford

Wishing you and yours Paschalia Gaudia, I fully adopt & confirm the title of Our Lady of the Angels, and if you ...... (?) can be ready for Monday April 4, I can bless & open the Church on that day. But if you cannot be ready for that day, I must propose the 7th as we have the Bishop's meeting on the 4th and 5th. Sunday April 3 is, of necessity spent at St. George's for the General Communion.

I write to Mr. Schofield about the accounts.

Shall we say April 7th & make ourselves ready?

If not, shall we say May 2nd as I confirm at Brighton May 1st.

Yours sincerely

+ Thomas Grant'

Letter from Bishop Grant to Thomas Gaisford

The Diocesan Directory, 1864/5 shows that on Sundays Fr. Schofield celebrated 'H. Comm at 8, Mass at 10.30, Lit, inst. and Bened. at 3.30. On Hds Mass at 9 and on Wds Mass at 8. On Frid in Lent Stats at 4.' The Rev. John McDonald was the Chaplain at Offington.

As the practice is at present, the information shown in this directory would no doubt have been forwarded to the Diocese during the latter part of the previous year.

On May 29 1864, the new church of Our Lady of the Angels was 'Privately' blessed and the first mass celebrated.

It has been noted that the website 'British History on Line' states in 'A History of the County of Sussex.....' thus, (*In Worthing*), 'A small Roman Catholic school was opened around 1864 .....'

The following document of authorisation by the Bishop was issued,

'The Church of St. Mary of the Angels, Worthing was undertaken on account of the increasing number of Catholic families visiting the town and neighbourhood. The generosity of the principal resident family has met the chief part of the expenses which have been incurred, and when the beautiful Church is nearly ready, it is found necessary to appeal to the goodness of friends, in order that the Church may be free from debt. The Local Priest, the Rev. Richard Schofield, is duly authorized to collect offerings for the Church and Mission, and we bless all who assist him.

St. George's March 25th, 1864

+ Thomas Grant

Fr. Schofield then produced the following document (money is shown in the old currency of £ (pounds) s (shillings.) and d (pence). There were 12 pennies to the shilling and twenty shillings to the pound),

'The Priest of the Mission of Worthing desires in this way to answer many queries which have been made, and to correct many misconceptions as to the resources and support of the Mission.

Though the Church and the Convent form one building and though the community attend the services of the New Church, the convent is altogether distinct from the Mission, and has special work of its own.

The neighbouring Chaplaincy of Offington House has a Chaplain, residing at Broadwater, and separate services. The Chapel is for the use of the household only, and not for the public, though permission is readily given to any Catholics who live on the other side of Offington, to attend the services.

The owner of Offington House generously subscribed 1,000 guineas for a Church in Worthing and to that sum has been added, by private subscription, about £400. The purchase of the site, and the building of the nave, have amounted to £1464 3s. 8d., and the subscriptions to £1457 9s. , leaving a deficiency of £6 14s. 8d.

When it was decided to open the Church this summer, and not wait for further subscriptions, the estimated expense of the Altar, furniture for the altar, sacristy, vestments, &c., was £230 ; of this sum, £177 16s. 4d. has been already expended in borrowed money, and to supply what was deficient, Vestments, furniture, &c., have kindly been lent, for present use.

A statement of the liabilities and receipts of the Mission shows,

	£	s.	d.
Balance due March 1st	6	14	8
Sundry accounts	177	16	4
	184	11	0
Subscriptions received	16	10	0
Balance due, Sept 1st	168	1	0

The whole of what is now received from the offertory and seat rents, is applied to the current expenses, and to the repayment of what has been expended on the interior. The church has been opened three months, and the receipts for offertory and sittings amount to £22 10s., and the current expenses, to £11, leaving £11 10s. available for the use of the Mission.

The Mission of Worthing – though the Church is filled with visitors in the Summer and Autumn – is not self supporting – in the Winter and Spring the amount received from the offertory does not exceed 5s. each Sunday.

The Local Priest makes this plain statement in the confident expectation that – without making further claims on an Individual who has already done so much – the present visitors, and those who recollect Worthing without a Mission, and without a Church, will readily and earnestly help in the good work of supporting the Mission, and in paying off the present debt of £168.1s.'

There is no copy of the original of this in the Archive held at St. Mary's.

Fr. John Henry Newman together with another priest from the Brompton Oratory in London arrived early in the day of November 10

1864, stayed the night at Offington and left late the following evening. It is difficult to believe that he did not visit the newly built church and once more meet Fr. Schofield. Fr. Newman was made John Henry, Cardinal Newman on May 12 1879 by Pope Leo XIII.

There follows a transcription of the pages of the Memoranda produced by Fr. Whiteside covering the years 1859 to 1869.

August 1859 - Count de Torres Diaz opened the mission in Augusta Place – Priest – Rev. Wollett

September 1859 – The portable altar and vestments taken to Offington House. – Major Gaisford continued the mission till November 9th 1862 in his house. During this time the priests were

Rev. J. Collingridge and Rev. Eugene Reardon

March 1860. Rev. J McDonald to (:-)

September 1861. (Then) Rev. M. J. Fannan

November 1862. – The Sisters of Notre Dame de Sion arrived.

November 9th 1862. – The first Mass celebrated at Wortley House. The mission removed from Offington to Worthing. Rev. M. J. Fannan chaplain at Offington House and also Missionary Priest of Worthing.

May 4th 1863. The Right Rev. Dr. Grant Bishop of the Diocese of Southwark laid the foundation stones of new church and convent.

An article from an unknown publication, held in parish archives filing, describing this event states,

'The foundation stone of a Catholic church and convent was laid on Monday, at Worthing, by the Right Rev. Dr. Grant, Bishop of Southwark. His Lordship, accompanied by Major Gaisford, arrived at the site of the future church and convent at 12 o'clock, and was received by the Very Rev. H. Canon Rymer, the Rev. M. Fannan, Pastor of the Mission, and the Revs. J. Butt, J. Sheehan, and R. Schofield. There were also present the Rev. Mother Superior and the sisters of the Convent of our Lady of Sion; many of the inhabitants of Worthing likewise attended. After a brief explanation of the ceremony, the Bishop, invested in his pontificals, and assisted by the clergymen present, proceeded to solemnly bless the stone and foundations, according to the rite prescribed by the church. At the end of the blessing, the Bishop being presented by Major Gaisford with a silver trowel, formerly placed the stone, which abuts on the convent wall. The Litany of the Saints was then said and the "Veni Creator" sung, after which his Lordship gave the Episcopal blessing to all present, and exhorted them to pray that Almighty God might deign to bless the work he had just begun, and protect the labourers from all accidents during the course of its erection.

The site of the church has been purchased by subscription. The entire length of the church will be 100 feet by 24. Only 50 feet of the nave, which Major Gaisford proposes to build at his own expense, will be erected at present. It is hoped the charity of the public will soon furnish means for the interior fittings and completion of the church. ..... The erection of the work is entrusted to Mr. Blaker, of Worthing, who will engage to finish by the 29th Sept. next."

February 10th 1864 The Rev. M. J Fannan left.

February 10th 1864. - The Rev. J. McDonald appointed chaplain of Offington House.

May 22nd 1864. – The last parish Mass celebrated at Wortley House.

May 29th 1864. – The new church of Our Lady of the Angels privately blessed and the first Mass celebrated.

September 9th 1864. – The new church of Our Lady (sic) of the Angels 'Solemnly' blessed by the Right Rev. Dr. Grant, Bishop of Southwark.

September 20th 1864. The Sisters of Notre Dame de Sion enter their new Convent.

The Reverend Richard Schofield had charge of the Mission from May 1863 to November 1864.

November 13th 1864. The Rev. J. McDonald took temporary charge of the Mission.

March 9th 1865 The Rev. Henry Bede Whiteside appointed to the charge of the Mission.

March 19th 1865 The Rev. H.B. Whiteside arrived and took charge of the Mission.

March 20th – The Presbytery furnished and inhabited by Priest, his mother and a servant.

April 7th The Rev H.B. Whiteside appointed by the Right Rev. Dr. Grant to bless private oratory of the convent and celebrate Mass therein once a week. Blessed Oratory and celebrated Mass therein this day leaving B. Sacrament in the Tabernacle.

Sample copy Memoranda page produced by Fr. Whiteside

The address of the presbytery, named St. Christopher's, was 39 Richmond Road.

Rev. H. B. Whiteside produced an Inventory of Mission church 'furniture' drawn up in April 1865.

The Bishop authorised the services Fr. Whiteside was allowed to celebrate in the following letter to him,

"Thomas Dei et Apostolice Sedis Gratia Episcopus Suthwarcensis

Benediction allowed at Worthing on

All Sundays

Days of Obligation and devotion

Octave of Corpus Christi and during the Octave

Last day of the year

One day in each week

   (signed) Thomas Episcopus"

Fr. Whiteside detailed the services he celebrated as follows,

'Order of Services from Easter Sunday April 16 1865 in the Church of Our Lady of the Angels Worthing.

Sunday – Holy Communion at 8 a.m., Mass at 10.30 a.m., Vespers, Benediction & Instruction 3.30p.m.

Weekdays – Mass every morning at 8.a.m.

Fridays in the Convent Oratory when the day is not engaged by festival etc.

Thursdays – Benediction at 3.30, Catechism for children immediately following'.

(It may be noted that again the name of the church is given as 'Our Lady of the Angels.' *The author's comment.*)

September 25th 1865, The Right Rev. Thomas Grant D.D. Bishop of Southwark made his visitation of this church and convent. He administered the Sacrament of Confirmation to nine persons and gave solemn benediction.

July 19th 1866, the Bishop visited Worthing once more administered the Sacrament of Confirmation and gave Benediction of the Most B. Sacrament.

As shown in the Directory of 1866/7, Father Whiteside celebrated

'On Sund and Hds H Comm at 8, Mass at 10.30, V and Bened at 3.30.

On wds Mass at 8. On Thurs Bened at 3.30, followed by Cat for children. On Frid in Lent Stats at 4.'

In modern language, this would read 'On Sundays and Holydays, Holy Communion at 8am, Mass at 10.30am; Vespers and Benediction at 3.30pm. On weekdays, Mass at 8am. On Thursdays, Benediction at 3.30pm, followed by Catechism for children. On Fridays in Lent, Stations of the Cross at 4pm'.

The Convent had been running for two years with only one weekly Mass celebrated in their oratory. For the Sisters to hear Mass daily, they had to leave the convent, walk round the corner and enter the church. A simpler weather-proof solution was considered and it was agreed that a 'Tribune' would be added to the church. What is now called the balcony was erected with access to it through a high level doorway from the convent building. This was especially useful for those Sisters who were frail or poorly.

Fr. Whiteside stated categorically that this addition was 'erected at the expense of the Sisters of Notre Dame for their own use and accommodation'. The same church architect and builder were used.

In later years, in reminiscences received by the author, mention was made of the use of the balcony by the Sisters. Young children noticed these strange people in their dark habits looking down through the railing and considered them 'very spooky'. At early Masses, the able bodied Sisters came down into the church through the door, now permanently locked, that can be seen on the south wall just past the Gaisford crypt, for the purpose of approaching the altar rails to receive communion. Due to the rule of fasting from midnight before receiving communion it was not distributed at the later morning Masses.

March 25th 1867 The Bishop visited the church on the Feast of the Annunciation. He blessed the Tribune and erected the Stations of the Cross in the church. These latter had been presented by Thomas Gaisford. He concluded his visit by giving Benediction. By this time the church had acquired a Processional Cross and brass torch-bearers paid for by subscription.

July 1867. The Very Rev. Theodore Ratisbonne arrived in Worthing on a visit to the Convent. As the convent had its own chapel, he would have celebrated Mass for the Sisters there. He would have had meetings with Fr. Whiteside and seen in more ways than one, how the church was joined spiritually and physically with the convent.

September 1867. A Baptismal Font was bought and placed near the front door. (At present it stands by the North East corner of the altar.)

September 22. 1867. The R.R. T. Grant Bishop made his Visitation of this church. He administered Confirmation and gave the Papal blessing.

December 6th 1867 Gas was laid on to the church. Evening services could now be held much more easily and these commenced at 7 p.m.

January 1868. A poor school was commenced at a small house no. 11 Cobden Road. Miss A. O'Brien took the management of it in September.

The last subject covered by the Memoranda by Fr. Whiteside refers to a document connecting Thomas Gaisford and St. Mary's indefinitely.

"Copy of Receipt.

Postage Stamp   Offington,   Worthing
Affixed   Nov. 13 1868
(usual practice)

Received from the Lord Bishop of Southwark £100 in payment for annexed account, and I hereby relinquish all further claims upon the Worthing Mission which I believe to be now quite free from debt.

The detailed accts. of the Mission are in the possession of the Priest at Worthing.

(signed)   T. Gaisford"

As a reply the Bishop stated thus,

Thomas, Dei et Apostolicae Sedis Gratia

Episcopus Suthwarcencis

"We declare that as Major Thomas Gaisford of Offington is the chief benefactor of the Church of the Holy Angels (*sic*) at Worthing, he and his children are entitled, after their respective deaths to be placed near the remains of his pious wife the Lady Emily Gaisford and of their child in the Vault constructed by him without the Sanctuary Rails of the said Church. May they whom Our Lord calls to Himself rest in peace, and may He spare the health and lives of those still remaining on this Earth.

St. George's Southwark. November 14 1868.

(signed)   Thomas Grant"

Was the Bishop unsure of the actual title of the church at the time of writing this document? Was it actually 'Our Lady of' or 'St. Mary of'? A very reliable source has explained that there is a Church Latin phrase for St. Mary i.e. Sancta Maria. There is no such equivalent for 'Our Lady'. Was that the reason or was there a considerable anti-Catholic feeling in the town generally to the development of church and convent and Our Lady may have been a very Catholic and disliked title?

The next entry may show this.

November 1868. A new Sanctuary corona lamp was presented to the church as an act of reparation in honor (*sic*) of the Blessed Sacrament for many insults that had been written and said against it in Worthing.

March 1869 A Statue of St. Joseph was presented to the church by Mrs. Delaney of the Hermitage, Ampleforth.

In 1870, the Bishop decided to move Fr. Whiteside from Worthing to change places with a Fr. James Purdon from Maidstone, Kent.

The last task for Fr. Whiteside was to write a letter to Fr. Purdon dated May 30 1870, explaining the situation the new priest would find at the Worthing Mission.

As referred to earlier, at that time it was still the practice to call the local churches governed by a Diocese a 'Mission church'. The title 'Parish' was not adopted until much later in 1918.

CHAPTER 9

The Early Purdon Years 1870 - 1899

The Rev. Fr. James Purdon was born near Hull in Yorkshire on December 18 1839. He was sent to the English College in Lisbon to study for the priesthood. He was ordained by Cardinal Ferieri, the Papal Nuncio to the Court of Lisbon on September 10 1863. The date of his arrival at Worthing can be fixed in some memories because it was the day that Charles Dickens died, July 9 1870 and Fr. Purdon was just thirty years old.

The Purdon years, recorded in a Journal covering the years 1870 until 1919 have been split into three sections.

The first section of the Journal begins with the letter to Rev. J. Purdon from Rev. H. Whiteside.

'Crescent Road. Worthing

May 30 1870

Dear Mr. Purdon

The Vicar General desires me to put myself in communication with you relating to the exchange which the Bishop has arranged between us.

At Worthing you will find not a large Presbytery, unfurnished, the duties of the Mission are light but continuous. At Easter the number of the souls within the limits of the district including the convent and the school was 170. There are constantly some visitors throughout the year for short periods. The season commences in July till October.

Besides the church and Convent which is contiguous to the Church: there is the residence of Major Gaisford who was the principal benefactor in building the church. He has a chapel in the house, and when the family is at home, which is generally for nine months of the year, he has the privilege of having the B. Sacrament reserved there. His arrangement with me was to remunerate me for each of the journeys I made at the rate of 10/- each time whilst he expected me to say Mass there twice a week.

There has been some difference between the Rev. Mother and me regarding the remuneration from the Community, about which for your own comfort it will be just as well to have a clear and explicit understanding.

The bench rents and offertories, taking the whole year round may average 25/- per week. There is no other source of income. But perhaps you will like to run down and see the place and have some talk. I should be glad to see you and can offer you a bedroom for a night or two. I should like you to inform about Maidstone, number of people, duties at the gaol, amount of income & how obtained, if this would not be giving you too much trouble.

I am,

Dear Mr. Purdon,

Yours very truly,

H. Whiteside."

On July 9 1870, the Rev. James Purdon took charge of the Worthing Mission.

The entry for November 11 1870 showed how within a few months the new priest was industriously active. A small schoolroom formed out of an old stable, was to serve as Chapel and School and was opened in John Street, Shoreham. Mass was celebrated by Fr. Purdon on that day.

'The ground for the site of the new church was given by the Rev. Wm. Wheeler, formerly Protestant Rector of the Town of New Shoreham. £800 being the amount of Mr. Wheeler's first donation with which sum the site has been purchased. Before the purchase of the site the Holy Mass was celebrated in a small & dingy house No.2 Surry Street.'

On January 10 1871 Bishop Grant was succeeded by Bishop James Danell who visited the mission later in the year on July 4 and gave the Sacrament of Confirmation in the church.

Although there is a gap with no entries for this time, as the next entry shows, Fr. Purdon had not been sitting on the laurels of Fr. Whiteside. He had been saying Mass at both Worthing and Shoreham and this continued until Shoreham became a Mission of its own.

Fr. Purdon's notes relate that in April 1873 new works to give the church a cruciform shape were commenced for the chancel, transept, sacristy, tower and school room. The expenses being entirely defrayed by Thomas Gaisford with the exception of some subscriptions for the school premises (£170). The entire expense of the building was approximately £2500. The bell and Altar rails were given by Miss Sarah Barker. There is a turret in the Bell tower and the diameter of the bell is 21.5 inches. It is hung in a 'B' frame and bears the inscription 'J. WARNER & SONS LONDON 1873 / S + / SOLI DEO GLORIA PAX HOMINIBUS. In 1970 it was recorded, by G.P. Elphick in 'Sussex Bells and Belfries', that there was a second bell hung in the covered passage from the Convent Chapel. The Altar of the Sacred Heart with the crucifix, tabernacle & candlesticks were given by Mr & Mrs Edmund Coffin as a thank offering for restoration of health to Mr. Coffin after a most serious illness. The Pulpit was given by Mr & Mrs. George Layer. Three handsome stained windows in the chancel were given by Thomas Gaisford, the founder & benefactor of the Mission, as a memorial of the Lady Emily Gaisford R.I.P. Under the column which supports the arches of the chapel of the Sacred Heart was placed an iron box containing a document & various religious objects together with stones taken from all the Catholic ruined edifices in the neighbourhood. The statue of the Sacred Heart was given by Miss Smart of Worthing.

An inscription on the base of an altar believed to be that dedicated to the Sacred Heart shows the following,

RECONNAISANCE

FEB XVI MDCCCLXXII

This date is transcribed as February 16 1872. It may show the date of the actual making of the altar, not the installation.

On November 12 1873, the new buildings were solemnly blessed & opened by Bishop J Danell and the Altar of the Sacred Heart was consecrated. The relics of Sts. Anastasius, Venantius and Victor were placed in the Altar. Sixteen priests assisted at the Pontifical High Mass. The young Duke of Norfolk with many other persons of distinction being present. Confirmation was administered in the afternoon by the Bishop.

In 1873, in what is now the church car park, a wooden hut was erected and used as rooms for a 'mixed school'. The original school was named St. Joseph's. In 1877 the school was enlarged to take 33 pupils whose parents paid 'school pence' for their attendance.

In 1875 the Mission of Shoreham gained Church, School and Presbytery these being paid for by (Augusta) Duchess of Norfolk and ˙ from this time Shoreham ceased to be a part of the Worthing Mission.

In March 1877 Miss Barker paid for a High Altar for St. Mary's together with a stone canopy and the Tabernacle was the gift of Thomas Gaisford. In July of that year a Statue of Our Lady and Child was given by Mrs. Alexander Ullathorne with a brass lamp to use before the Altar of the Sacred Heart.

Photograph of Fr J Purdon

A piece of land measuring about 160 feet (50m) in length & 65 feet (20m) in depth at the West side of the Presbytery was purchased in 1877. A portion of the land which overlapped the Convent grounds was given in exchange for the site of the South transept. The expenses were defrayed by the Bishop, Thos. Gaisford and Fr. Purdon. The amount was £175 for the land alone: the walls etc being paid for by Fr. Purdon and E. Coffin, and Alex Ullathorne (£5 each).

A new Class Room & Offices were added to the school at this time costing about £120.

In June 1878 two iron & brass coronals were given by Edmund Coffin.

In 1879, St. Joseph's school received an annual grant from the Education Authorities. In that year, the organ having been hired (for four years by the Rev. J. Purdon), was bought by public subscription. The price of the instrument in its original state was £120. The names of the subscribers and the amount of the subscriptions shown as follows:

Duke of Norfolk, £3, Thos. Gaisford Esq., £33, Lady Alice Gaisford, £10, The Mother General, £10, Mr. & Mrs. E. Coffin, £15, Mr. Mangles, £10, Mr. Wasteneys, £5, Mr. Ullathorne, £5, Mrs. Mansel, £5, Mr. Haslacher, £2, Mr. Flynn, £1, Capt. H. Gaisford, £1, Collection in church, £5, Mr. Neale, 10/6, Mr. Pritchard Rayner, 10/6. Total £106.1.0.

The balance was given by Fr. Purdon. Several additions were made to the instrument costing about £20 which sum was also paid by Fr. Purdon.

Fr. Purdon's Journal appears to relate solely to the history of St. Marys development as a building. It does not mention a sad but important happening that occurred in September 1879 recorded in the Kent and Sussex Courier of October 1 thus,

'Major Gaisford of Offington .... has sustained a sad bereavement in the death of his eldest son, Captain (Horace Charles) Gaisford, of the Grenadier Guards which occurred on Saturday week. The internment in accordance with the rites of the Roman Catholic Church, took place on Thursday. The body of the deceased lay in the Church of St. Mary of the Angels, Crescent Road, on Wednesday night, and at eleven o'clock on Thursday morning the Bishop of Southwark (Dr. Danell) celebrated the solemn Requiem Mass. .... In the celebration of Mass the Bishop was assisted by the Very Rev. Canon Butt, of Arundel; the Rev. N. Crispin, of Brighton (deacon), the Rev. – Moynihan (sub deacon); the Revs. J. Purdon and – Roe (assistant deacons); and the Rev. Keatinge, of Arundel, who officiated as Master of the Ceremonies.'

In September 1881, two fine Statues carved in wood, one of St. Joseph and one of Blessed Virgin Mary, were given to the church by Fr. Purdon.

On June 14 1881, Bishop Danell died. He was succeeded by Bishop Robert Coffin on May 25 1882.

In August 1882, works were commenced on the building of a new transept and chapel for St. Joseph. (*Now used as Blessed Sacrament Chapel*). The whole expense was paid for by Thos. Gaisford, the generous benefactor & founder of the Mission. The site on which the chapel stands was given in exchange by the convent, for the site of their orphanage. A lamp and small altar in wood for the statue of St. Joseph were given by the Rev. Mother General, Mere Rose.

Also installed in that year were two stained glass memorial windows put in the church in memory of Mr. Gaisford's eldest son and two other children who died in infancy. They depicted St. Charles Borromeo and an Angel Guardian.

In 1883, Bishop Coffin made his first visit to Worthing as Bishop and gave confirmation to 39 candidates, 23 being converts. It is believed he was a relative of one of the parishioners of St. Mary's.

Sept. 30 1884   Mrs Alex Ullathorne gave a pair of Candelabra for St. Joseph's chapel.

On April 6 1885, Bishop Coffin died to be succeeded by Bishop John Butt on June 26 1885.

On July 18 1885, work began to add two extra rooms to the Presbytery, which was paid for by subscription, the amount being rather more than £290. A small tin box containing sacred medals was placed in the foundations by Fr. Purdon.

The entry of July 28 1885 gives a list of the Subscriptions paid to defray the cost of adding the extra Presbytery rooms:

G. Loyer (?) £5, Bishop Butt, £35, Mrs. Mansel, £5, Lady Alice Gaisford, £5, A Ullathorne, £10, Mrs. Coffin, £20, Mrs. Doe, £5, Mrs. Riley, £5, Mr. Digby, £5, Rev. Mother, £10.

Total realised £105.   Expenses £285.

The entry of Aug 5 1885 details a letter to a Mr. Rees reference a loan offered to Rev. Fr. J Purdon.

'Dear Mr. Rees,

I thank you more sincerely than I can express for your kindness in advancing that £100 of the £200 you so kindly offered to lend me.

I think that there should be some clear understanding in writing relative to this transaction; so to recapitulate what we have already said, the matter stands thus.

With the consent of the two trustees of the Mission property an addition of two rooms has been made to the presbytery. You have kindly advanced the sum of £100 and the £200 promised to be repaid by instalments in the space of ten years.

The advance has been made to me but with the proviso that it is to be a debt on the Catholic Mission of Worthing to be paid off in ten years: this I have clearly laid before the Bishop, Dr. Butt, & he has given his entire consent to that so that in case of my death or removal my successor, or the Bishop, will be the responsible person to whom application for repayment must be made for the whole or part still remaining of the sum borrowed.

Hoping this explanation will cover all the conditions of the arrangement.

I am always

Sincerely yours

(Signed) J.Purdon'

There followed a copy of Bishop Butt's letter relative to this note.

St. George's Cathedral

August 6 1885

Dear Fr. Purdon

I sent your letter to Mr. Rees, as I had no alteration to suggest.

Yours sincerely in Xt

+ John Butt

Fr. Purdon shows how important the repayment of a debt was in the wording of the above letter and how he included details in the Journal of each repayment realising the successful completion of this business.

Repayments of £20 were made each year from 1885 until 1894.

Fr. Purdon added a copy of a publication showing that there were strong anti-catholic feelings held by some Worthing residents. It is an article from the 'English Churchman and St. James' Chronicle' July 22 1886.

'The Protestant town of Worthing is about to be invaded by the Romanisers, and the Rev. Gilbert C. F. J. Moor has been selected as leader in the approaching battle. The new Church of St. Andrew's is in course of erection at Worthing, and Mr. Moor has been chosen as the new Vicar. This champion of the anti-

Protestant movement is a member of the principal Ritualistic Societies.

The secret Society of the Holy Cross, which circulated that grossly indecent guide for Father Confessors, "The Priest in Absolution," and requires all its members to go to Confession, and offer the Mass, has the name of Mr. Moore (sic) in the list of its Brethren.

The Confraternity of the Blessed Sacrament, established solely to propagate the idolatrous doctrine of the Real Presence, and the "blasphemous fable" of the Sacrifice of the Mass, has his name on its 'Roll of Priests-Associate'.

He is also a member of the English Church Union, which is ever foremost in trying to crush all existing authority in the Church of England, and is well known as the shameless defender of Ritualistic rebels.

Moreover, Mr. Moor has just resigned the Curacy of St. Augustine's, Kilburn, where, alas, the Ritual law of the Church of England is broken with impunity. Such is the new Vicar of St. Andrew's, Worthing. He will, doubtless, be a very unwelcome addition to the clergy of the town. Husbands who do not wish their wives and children to attend the Confessional, would do well to keep them out of the reach of Mr. Moor's influence, and on no account should they consent to their attending his services'.

(An interesting note, reference the Anti-Catholic article shown above. The Dowager Lady Loder – who is mentioned several times below as a benefactor of St. Mary's - gave £500 to Rev. Gilbert Moor as a donation towards the building of a parish-room at St. Andrew's Anglican Church.)

In 1887, storm doors were put up, paid for by subscriptions.

In 1888 three stained glass windows in the north and south transepts were given by Mrs. Alexander Ullathorne.

The Morning Post of November 22 1889 reported an event that took place three days earlier,

'The marriage of Mr. Julian Gaisford, eldest son of Mr. Gaisford of Offington, Sussex, and the late Lady Emily Gaisford, and Miss Bertha Riddell, eldest daughter of Mr. Riddell of Cheeseburn Grange, Northumberland took place in the private chapel at Cheesburn Grange, on Tuesday. The ceremony was performed by the Right Rev. Dr. Riddell, Bishop of Northampton, assisted by the Rev. W. E. Baron and Fr. Gavin, S.J. Bridesmaids, Miss Riddell, Miss Gaisford (sic) and Miss May Gaisford and Miss Egerton. Mr. Philip (sic) Gaisford, brother to the bridegroom, acted as best man ......'

With the death of Horace in 1879, Julian as eldest son would later take over the Gaisford House and Estate at Offington and become a benefactor of the church as his father did before him.

On November 25 1891 a set of 6 fine brass candlesticks for the high Altar were given by Mrs. Delme Radcliffe & Miss Moxon as a thank offering.

In 1892, extra benches were given to the church by Mr. Gaisford.

The Journal includes details of a letter from Fr. Purdon.

" Worthing

June 8 1895

My dear Mr. Gaisford

I thank you, more deeply than my words can express, for your kind note & generous offering.

It does indeed seem impossible that so long a time has passed! To me they have been twenty five years of happiness without a single serious flaw.

Though much more might have been done, with God's blessing and the generosity of benefactors we have not been idle as the following figures will show.

Additions to Church, Schools; Organ; High Altar; Side Altar; Windows; Candlesticks; Pulpit; Additions to Presbytery; Garden & Walls; Convent enlargement; Shoreham Site, Church, School & Presbytery; Convalescent Home. (*All individual figures noted, totalling £16,992.*)

These are some items not speaking of large sums used on the services of the church & furniture of mission etc., etc.

I am truly grateful to God for having inspired so many good souls to do so much in a very quiet way.

I thank you & your family for their unchanging kindness to me in so many, many ways.

I am always very gratefully yours,

J. Purdon"

Sometime in 1896 a Stained Glass window was given by Mrs. Kenelm Digby in memory of her husband.

A draft of a letter from T. Gaisford to, it is believed, Mr. E. Patching of Patching & Co., referring to his burial in the Gaisford Vault in St. Mary of the Angels. Some wording is indecipherable.

In 1895 Mr. Verrall was the Town Clerk at Worthing.

Offington Jan 14 1897

'Dear Sir

The late Mr. R. C. Blaker who built, for me, the R.C. Church at Worthing also constructed a vault or Founders Tomb as shown in enclosed plan. The tomb can hold only 3 coffins and the requirements of Home Office as to external ventilation have been complied with.

On the death of Lady Emily Gaisford Nov 6 1868, I wrote to Mr. Verrall as to the Burial, unfortunately I cannot find both my note or his answer which were both preserved and about 4 years ago, I spoke to Mr. Verrall but probably this correspondence has not been found.

I do not anticipate that objections would be made if I desire to be buried in the grave of my late wife but I would like to have some assurance that I can safely leave a written memorandum to that effect.

Will you kindly go to the Church, Fr. Purdon would give you any information but he was not in Worthing when the nave of the Church was built and having seen Mr. .... (illegible) I should be much obliged if you would speak to Mr. Verrall.

I may add that 2 of my sons have been buried in the cemetery since 1868. They were neither of them children of the late Lady E. Gaisford.

Yours faithfully

G.'

There follows a letter that indicates quite clearly that at that time Thomas Gaisford was considered the 'founder' of the church.

From Edward C. Patching to T. Gaisford Esq. J.P. Offington.

'Jany 29 1897

Dear Sir

After several interviews with Mr. Verrall I am in a position to write and tell you, that no difficulty need be apprehended as to the future use of the Founders Vault in the R.C. Church in Worthing, provided the Home Secretary's consent is forthcoming at such time as it may be required.

I have been up to the Church and the Rev. J. W. Purdon very kindly showed me the position of vault and explained the whole position to me.

I enclose your plan of the Church and I have taken a tracing of the portion that will be useful to me at any future time.

Yours faithfully

Edward C. Patching.'

On April 12 1897, Bishop Butt resigned, and the Coadjutor Bishop, Bishop Bourne succeeded him.

On June 29 1897, Bishop Bourne made his first canonical visitation and administered the Sacrament of Confirmation.

The entry for November 8 1897 tells of important improvements being made in the cleaning, match-boarding and varnishing of the whole of the Church and roof repairs undertaken, the whole of the expense being paid by Thomas Gaisford.

On December 17 1897, the Rev. Mother General presented a new Statue of the Sacred Heart.

On April 18 1898, the repairs to the roof were commenced; this work was ordered by Mr. Thomas Gaisford at the same time the improvements and repairs were done inside the church, delay was occasioned by the want of tiles and the work was further postponed on account of Lent and Holy Week. The expense was to be met by the claim on the estate, about £500.

On August 14 1898 a new stone reredos, being a copy of that in Chichester Cathedral, was solemnly inaugurated at the evening service. It was the joint gift of the Dowager Lady Loder and Mr. & Mrs. Digby, the cost being £453. The architect was Mr. F. A. Walters and Messrs. Earp & Holts of Lambeth installed the reredos. Under the statue of St. Wilfred was placed a bronze medal with a fine portrait of Leo XIII, the reigning Pope, under St. Richard's statue, a coin of the realm, dated 1898.

It can be seen from the British History on Line website that the average attendance at St. Joseph's school at this time was 84 pupils.

In August 1899 a silver plated lamp was given to the church by Miss B. Davies-Cooke in memory of her sister Kathleen Davies-Cooke.

Again, sadly, in covering the physical development of the Mission, the Journal has no mention of any events marking the start of a new century. It may be assumed that the parish would have had some service of thanksgiving at the end of the year or a similar service of celebration at the start of the New Year.

View into St. Joseph's chapel after 1923
the year of Canon Purdon's death.

CHAPTER 10
A Farewell to Thomas Gaisford - 1898

On February 26 1898, Fr. Purdon wrote in his Journal that 'Thomas Gaisford, the founder of & generous benefactor to the Mission, died at Offington. R. I. P. A sad day, and an irreparable loss to the Mission and many others'.

On March 2 1898, he again included the fact that 'Thomas Gaisford was buried in his own vault as principal benefactor of the Mission'. The Mass was said by Rev. J. Purdon, the friend and confessor for twenty-seven years of the deceased, and the Priest of the Mission. Bishop Bourne, assisted and gave the absolution. Great public sympathy and respect was shown in the Town, and at the funeral; all the papers giving the most truthful and highest praise of the deceased, both in his private and public character'.

On March 2 1898 the Worthing Gazette reported,

'The deceased gentleman, whose health had been declining a considerable time – several months having elapsed since he last attended the Worthing Bench to discharge his magisterial duties – became a victim to influenza about a week ago. Pneumonia supervened, and although every effort was made to restore him to health, he sank under that formidable disease.

A large-hearted and broad-minded man, he never strained the law to the detriment of anyone who had the misfortune to be brought before him, and if he strove to hold evenly the scales of justice, any redeeming feature in a case was marked by a compassionate leniency in his decision. In 1890 he filled the vacancy of Chairman of the Worthing Bench.

Last evening the body of the deceased was removed from Offington to the church reposing beneath a catafalque and surrounded by lighted candles. A brass Calvary cross extended the full length of the coffin.

A 'founders' grave was appropriated for him in the aisle of the church, and here, some years since, sepulchre was found for Lady Emily Gaisford and an infant child. It was necessary to obtain the direct sanction of the Home Secretary for today's ceremony; but now that the grave has closed over him for whose use it was specially designed, it will be no more opened.

Commencing at eleven o'clock the service lasted an hour and a half.

The celebrant was the Rev. James Purdon, and it was carried out in the presence of the Right Rev. Dr. Bourne, Bishop of Southwark.

There were a number of acolytes in robes, and incense was freely used. The service was throughout in Latin, the music being rendered by the choir in the screened gallery above. As the solemn and impressive function neared its close, Dr. Bourne made his way to a seat placed for him in the aisle immediately fronting the coffin, wearing now a most elaborate robe.

The Bishop both censed and sprinkled the coffin; and then at a sign from Mr. E. C. Patching, (who together with Mr. F. W. Patching was present to superintend the arrangements), the bearers stepped silently forward and lowered the coffin into the grave during the Benedictus, and the service closed with the words "Resquiescat in Pace".

Then the impressive strains of the "Dead March" burst forth from the organ, and the solemnly picturesque ceremony was at an end, most of the mourners and spectators filing past the grave before quitting the church'.

Inside Church - 1938 extension showing Gaisford family vault

CHAPTER 11

The Middle Purdon Years 1900 - 1914

On April 5 1900, important additions to the church were commenced including a new aisle and baptistery and enlargement of the Porch and Sacristy. The whole expense (about £1000) being paid by the Dowager Lady Loder, the architect was Mr. Walters the same who designed the reredos. The work was carried out by Messrs. Patching & Co.

The Journal states that on September 9 1900 Fr. Purdon blessed new benches as additions to the church. They were given by (the new) Mr. & Mrs. Gaisford, Mr. & Mrs. Digby, Mr. Joseph Mifsud, Mrs. Johnson, Miss Davies Cooke and Mr. McGedy.

On December 15 1900, two stained glass windows were placed in the new baptistery. 'The Baptism of Our Lord' was given by Mrs. Mary Ann Rogers, the faithful housekeeper and 'The Visitation of B. V. M.' by Fr. Purdon.

In 1901, carved oak chancel benches and kneelers were given by the Dowager Lady Loder. (In 1899 she lived in Beach House).

In 1902, the west wall of the Sanctuary was decorated in fresco with statuary, the expense being defrayed by the Dowager Lady Loder, the designs drawn by F. A. Walters Esq., 37 Old Queen Street, Westminster.

Again in October 1902, a beautiful Altar, dedicated to the Holy Souls, as a memorial shrine to the deceased Catholic relatives of the Dowager Lady Loder was erected in the North Aisle, at her ladyship's sole cost. The designs by F. A. Walters the stone work by Hatch of Vauxhall. Brasses by Hardman & Co. Cost £815. Lady Loder may have filled the gap left by the death of Thomas Gaisford some years before.

In October 1902, two fine wrought iron chancel screens given by Mrs. T. K. Digby as a thanksgiving offering for the restoration to health of her youngest son, Claude. Cost £88.

On July 12 1904, Bishop Amigo made his canonical visitation and gave confirmation to 34 candidates.

In September 1904, a beautiful carved wood rood beam was placed in the church, a gift of the 'generous benefactrix' the Dowager Lady Loder. The design by Mr. F. A. Walters included three central figures that were made in Holland and copied ancient ones existing in the Collegiate Church at Louvain, Belgium. In October of that year the decoration of the chancel was finished, the expense being defrayed by the Dowager Lady Loder again, under the direction of Mr. F. A. Walters.

During the years 1904 – 1906, Mrs H. Haywood made several valuable presents, a solid gold cross set with whole pearls; a dove of the same valuable make; a gold Cross with solid pearls for the Monstrance, and the dove is set in the ..... of the Ciborium cover, a quantity of Altar linen and a solid silver Ciborium.

Sometime in 1907, Mrs Haywood presented to the Mission a pair of Spanish brass candlesticks to be placed with the statue of St. Joseph. All richly embroidered work for albs in red and white taken from piece in drawn work for albs. (*sic*)

On October 27 1907, Bishop Amigo made his second canonical visitation and administered the Sacrament of Confirmation to 48 candidates.

On November 15 1907, the Dowager Lady Loder died, R.I.P. She had been a convert to the Catholic Church for about ten years and from that time a member of the Worthing congregation; during that time several important and costly additions were made in the church which are described elsewhere in this history.

On December 8 1907, Mrs. Mansel of 1 Knightsbridge Mansions, London, made a beautiful and costly present of a shrine and statue of Our Lady the design was given by Mr. Walters to whose care and judgement all the recent improvements which have been done in the church for the last ten years have been entrusted. (Cost) £201.

On May 5 1908 an important announcement was made. At the Diocesan Synod, the Bishop Dr. Amigo constituted the Mission of Our Lady of Angels, Worthing a 'Missionary Rectorate' and appointed the Rev. J. Purdon as the first Missionary Rector. To celebrate the event the Rev. C. Conley Clarke gave two fine oil paintings to the church.

At this time it was recognised that Fr. Purdon had completed, single-handedly, thirty eight years work in church and parish with ever increasing numbers and responsibilities and he must have help.

Thus it was that in September 1908, Fr. Purdon ended his solitary work at St. Mary's as from that date the Reverend John Fichter became assistant priest and also chaplain to St. Mary's Home.

By 1909 Mr. Julian had become Commander Julian Charles Gaisford-St. Lawrence, RN, DL, JP.

On March 17 1909, The Aberdeen Journal reported that:-

'Charles Gaisford of Offington, Sussex, will succeed in the ownership of the Howth estates from Lord Howth. (His maternal uncle). Mr. Gaisford is the eldest son of the late earl's eldest sister, Lady Emily Gaisford.'

This was actually 'Julian' Charles Gaisford of Offington.

J.C. Gaisford St. Lawrence J.P.

This resulted in the senior Gaisford family leaving Worthing and removing to Howth, just outside Dublin. The Gaisford connection with St. Mary's that had been so close for exactly fifty years was ending. He sold the village of Bulkington in Wiltshire, owned by the Gaisford family since, at the earliest, 1839.

However, it was remembered in several ways with the naming of what was Gaisford High School and St. Lawrence and Bulkington Avenues.

On December 8 1909, Mrs. Mansell presented a fine pair of columns to be placed at the shrine of Our Lady, given by her this day in 1907.

By 1910 St. Joseph's had developed into an infant and mixed school.

On December 6 1910, Bishop Amigo visited Worthing to administer Confirmation.

The Journal recalls that on October 6 1912, the Bishop made his third canonical visitation and administered the Sacrament of Confirmation to thirty converts (?) and others.

On September 19 1913, Fr. Purdon celebrated the Golden Jubilee of his priesthood. After the High Mass sung by Fr. Purdon a meeting was held in the Convent at which several priests and a large number of the congregation assisted. A testimonial was given consisting of a purse with £260, one hundred of which was given by Mrs. Mansell; considerable sums were given by persons not residing in the Mission. The Holy Father was approached by both the Bishop and the Convent and sent his blessing in the form of a special document handsomely framed in Vellum through the Convent authorities. The priests who assisted were the Right Rev. Monsignor Connelly, Very Rev. Canon Murmane, Revs. E. Butt, R. Christlade, Sulivan(?), and J. Fichter, assistant priest of the Mission. Exceedingly pleasant references to the event were given in the Local and London papers.

Sept. 9 1914   The Golden Jubilee of the Mission was held and to commemorate the occasion the church was thoroughly renovated, about £30 being spent on this object. Fr. Purdon sang High Mass of thanksgiving assisted by Frs. Chrislade of Walworth and Fichter, assistant priest at the Mission.

View of Sanctuary and Main Altar prior to 1940's

CHAPTER 12

St. Mary's and the First World War

Just over four weeks before St. Mary's celebrated her Golden Jubilee, on August 4 1914, the United Kingdom declared war on Germany, an event that was to have devastating effects on the country.

Although St. Mary's, Worthing, did not have what may be called a large congregation, there were twenty men who either lived in Worthing or had strong connections to the town and lost their lives.

What can be discovered of these people is described below.

A stone memorial is mounted on the exterior of the East Wall of the church listing the parishioners of St. Mary's who lost their lives in the First World War.

It could be said that our parish was fortunate that there are only twenty names shown on the memorial. They range from a Private in the Royal Sussex Regiment and a Lieutenant in the Royal Flying Corps., to a Lieut. Colonel in the Seaforth Highlanders.

Their names are listed below. Only initials of first names are shown on the tablet. The name has been ascertained for each man and, where possible, the Army information on each man has been found. As thirteen of them have only one initial this task was rather difficult.

The Census of 1891, 1901 and 1911 was examined to find as much detail as possible about each serviceman to try to ascertain the correct person is listed below. There is definite proof for only a small percentage of these people. In the other cases it cannot be achieved without some doubt and where there are not too many, alternatives are added.

They are,

W(alter) D(ouglas) Aston Captain, Cambridgeshire Regiment, 1st Bn., died 02.11.17, died of wounds suffered during Passchendaele, aged 35 and is buried in Lijsenthoek Military Cemetery, Grave XX1.FF.13.

He was the son of Mr & Mrs Walter Aston of 'Riverside' Shelley Road, Worthing. His wife was C.O. Aston of 1228 Ohio Street, Lawrence, Kansas, USA. He was born at Tarporley, Cheshire and was an LL.M., a Fellow of Downing College, Cambridge, and also held offices of Steward Librarian and Lecturer in Law at that College.

C(harles William) Boniface   Number GS/351, Private, 2nd Bn., Royal Sussex Regiment, 1st Divn., Reservist.   British Expeditionary Force. Died 25.09.15 during battle of Loos, aged 37 and is commemorated on the Loos Memorial, Panel 69 to 73. His death was recorded by an officer, 'At the time he was wounded, he was cutting the enemy's wire. He was wounded in three places, then a fourth struck him in the head.'

In 1911, Charles William Boniface, born in Poling, was 33 living in 16 Jubilee Terrace, Penfold Road, Worthing and was a Domestic Gardener at Sion Convent. He left a wife Amy Mates and a five year old son, Frederick Charles who were living at 31 Penfold Road.

C(harles Percy) Campbell (On 1901 Census) Number 78994, Private, 4th Bn., Northumberland Fusiliers, enlisted Brighton, Sussex, died 27.05.18. He is commemorated on the Soissons Memorial.

In 1901 & 1911 Charles Percy lived in 33 Montgomery Street, Hove, and was a schoolboy born in 1899. He was the son of Dence Weller and Alice Sarah Campbell of The Beaufort Hotel, 175 Queen's Park Road, Brighton at time of death.

Or:-

C(olin) Campbell (On 1901 Census)   born 1896, St. Leonard's, Sussex, living at 5 Linton Road, Hastings Holy Trinity, Sussex. Parents Duncan and Charlotte both born in Hastings.

J(ohn) Cassidy   Number S/1792, Private, 7th Bn., Seaforth Highlanders, died 25.09.15.   He is commemorated on the Loos Memorial, Panel 112 to 115.

In 1901 there was an Alice Cassidy who was a Servant of a Grogan family living at Tovil House, 1 Latimer Terrace, Worthing. She was the only Cassidy in Worthing on the census of both 1891 and 1901.

In 1911 there was a twelve year old schoolboy named John Cassidy living at 28 King Street, Portsea. Both parents and sister, William, Jessie and Kathleen were born in Worthing.   His father was a Bootmaker.

J(ames) Coleman   Number G/12327, Private, 9th Bn., Royal Sussex Regt., killed in action 12.08.17, aged 32.   Buried in Hooge Crater Cemetery, Grave X. B. 4.

On 1891 Census, there is a James, one year old son of James, a Carter born in 1849, and Annie, born in 1851, of Ham Lane, Broadwater.

There are one hundred and three other 'J' Coleman's listed.

Jeremiah Joseph Driscoll Number 296386, A.B., R.N., Stoker 1st Class, HMS Indefatigable, died at the Battle of Jutland at 4.03pm 31.05.16. He is commemorated on the Plymouth Naval Memorial. His name is on a brass plaque found in the back of a deep cupboard in the church. It is now mounted in the church.

On 1891 Census, Jeremiah Joseph Driscoll was 9 living with his parents Jeremiah and Bridget in 2 Newlands Street, Worthing and was a scholar.

On the 1901 Census he is shown living in the 'Vicarage' with Fr. James Purdon and is a Domestic Servant. It may be considered that the record of this seaman's death on the only plaque of its kind in the church was due to the closeness of the employer to his employee.

There is no record of him found on the 1911 Census. Was he already a seaman by that date and at sea?

E(dward John) Elms Number G/7858, Private, Royal Sussex Regt., 2nd Bn., died 22.11.16, aged 28. He is commemorated on the Thiepval Memorial, Pier and Face 7 C.

In 1911 Edward John was a lodger in 127 Southfield Road, Worthing. He was then single and a Jobbing Gardener.

J(ohn) C(uthbert) Finlay Captain, B Coy., 26th (Tyneside Irish) Bn., Northumberland Fusiliers, died 23.11.16. He is commemorated on the Cite Bonjean Military Cemetery, Armentieres, 111. B. 2.

In 1911 John Cuthbert was a boarder in 4 Southdown Terrace, Lyndhurst Road, Worthing. He was 29 years old, a single man who was a Laundry Manager. He was born in Newcastle upon Tyne. He was the brother of Mr. F. Finlay of 13 Fairfield Road, West Jesmond, Newcastle upon Tyne.

E(ric) W(illiam) Fullilove Number PO/15637, Private, Royal Marine Light Infantry, died 23.08.20 presumably of wounds. He is buried in Worthing (Broadwater) Cemetery, Grave A6. 8. 11.

In 1911 Eric William was a thirteen year old school/errand boy living with his parents in Kingsbury House, West Street, Worthing. His father was a Naval Pensioner acting as a Bath Attendant.

W(alter) T(homas) Gaisford   Lieutenant Colonel, Seaforth Highlanders, 7th Bn., died 25.09.15, aged 44. His body was never found. He is commemorated on the Loos Memorial, Panel 112 to 115 and Scottish National War Memorial, Edinburgh Castle. It was the first day of this battle.

Walter Thomas was the son of Thomas Gaisford and his last wife, Lady Alice Mary. He was born in Sussex.

On 1911 census he is shown at Broadwater aged 39, single, with a servant and two visitors.

In 1911 he was also shown posted with his regiment to Chanbattia, India. His home, at the time of his death, was Hambleton Lodge, Chackmore, Radclive, Bucks. He was unmarried.

The battle of Loos was the largest British offensive mounted in 1915, on the Western front during World War 1. It commenced on the 25th September, lasted nineteen days and achieved nothing. The 7th Battalion attacked the Hohenzollern Redoubt, South West of Auchy. The Gaisford family was allowed to erect a memorial to Walter Thomas. It consisted of a large canopied crucifix positioned in the church forecourt. It was removed in the 1938 changes to the church. All that remains is a memorial block duly inscribed which can be seen in the courtyard of the church.

W(alter) P(hilip) G(ordon) Harrold   Number SD/2698, Lance Sergeant, 13th Bn, Royal Sussex Regt., died 03.09.16, aged 18. Commemorated on the Thiepval Memorial, Pier and Face 7 C. Before his death he had already been awarded the Military Medal. The citation for the award read 'While our troops were leaving the parapet, Sgt. Harrold was buried by the parapet being blown down by a shell. He was extricated, and although shaken, rallied the nearest men, took them over the parapet and led them into the German trench.'

In 1911 he was the son of Charles Henry Harrold living at 12 Montague Place, Worthing. The notification of his death went to his father at 55 Heene Road, Worthing.

F(rank) Hof   Number 87935, Gunner, 86 Brigade, Royal Field Artillery, discharged 13.02.18, due to wounds, awarded Silver War Badge, 14.02.18. Died of wounds 12.07.1918. Commemorated in United Kingdom Book of Remembrance.

In 1911 he lived at 50 Barrowgate Road, Chiswick with wife Flora and son Herbert aged 5 and Lillian aged 3. He was a Domestic Gardener and Nurseryman. His father Francis Hof died, aged 66, at 7 Orme Road, Worthing, in 1914.

Frank Hof died, in 1918, aged 40, in Willesden, Middlesex. Ref. 3A 225.

E(dward) M(olyneux) Knapp (DCM)   Number 1403, Sergeant, C. Coy., 1st/15th Bn., London Regiment (Prince of Wales' Own Civil Service Rifles). Died 07.08.16 aged 33.   Commemorated on the Thiepval Memorial, Pier and Face 13 C. Son of the late Dr. Edward Molyneux and Isabella Rosalind Knapp.

In 1901, a bank clerk in Southampton, living with mother and family.

In 1911 Edward and Mother Isabella Rosalind were living in Croydon, Surrey.   Mother born in Pimlico, London, Edward in Ross, Herefordshire. He was a bank clerk in Croydon.

B(ert) Munday   Number 939, Lance Sergeant, 2nd Bn., Lancashire Fusiliers, died 03.05.15. (? Possibly). He was serving as a Butler. Commemorated on the Ypres (Menin Gate) Memorial, Panel 8 and 12.

On the C.W.G.C. site, he is noted as the son of the late John and Annie Munday.

In 1911 there was a Bertram Alfred, born 1894, son of Charles Munday (Hotel Keeper) and Anni (sic) living and working as a single Barman at the Warwick Hotel, Warwick Street, Worthing.

There are five other possible soldiers noted on the C.W.G. Comm. site.

F(rederick) Munday   Number 8673, Sergeant, 1st. Bn., Worcester Regiment, died 06.07.16. Commemorated on the Thiepval Memorial, Pier and Face 5A and 6 C.

In 1901 there was a Frederick M, aged 14, living at 31 Market Street, Worthing with family and was a Stationers Errand Boy. Mrs. Munday was the informant of both these deaths when the Town memorial was produced. It can be assumed that the two soldiers were related.

In 1911 there was a Frederick, aged 24, born in Worthing, living at 27 Keere Street, Lewes with Amy Wilson and her son Mark.

There are seven other possible soldiers of that name noted on the C.W.G. Comm. site.

D(aniel) Murphy (?) Number S/22856, Private, 7th. Bn., Seaforth Highlanders, died 19.12.17. Buried in Gouzeaucourt New British Cemetery Grave IX.A.B.

In 1901 aged 18, plumber, (son of Daniel, born 1843 in Ireland, Pensioner Chief Boatman Ct), at 142, Back of Montague St., Worthing.

Fifteen other 'D. Murphy' possibilities on C.W.G. Commission site who are not included here.

H(enry) E(ward) Murray MM Number L/7662, Lance Corporal, 12th (Prince of Wales' Royal) Lancers, died of wounds, 03.04.18. aged 27. Buried in St. Sever Cemetery Extension, Rouen, P. IX. O.6A. Husband of Mrs H. E. Murray of The Manor House, Littlehampton, son of Mr & Mrs George Murray of North View, Courtlands, Goring by Sea, Sussex. He was born in Shepherd's Bush, London.

P(hilip) Pearce Number 183356(PO), A.B., R.N., HMS "Princess Irene", b. 21.12.79, died 27.05.15. aged 35. Commemorated on Portsmouth Naval Memorial, Plaque 8. Killed by internal explosion of vessel off Sheerness. Body not recovered for burial. Born in Shoreham, Father the late Thomas Francis Pearce and Mother, Amelia, 12 Wenban Road, Worthing, who was notified of death.

W(alter) F(eldwicke) Pollard Number 23245, Rifleman, 4th Bn., 3rd New Zealand Rifle Brigade, died of wounds 30.12.16. aged 25. Buried in Estaires Communal Cemetery Extension, III(?) L. (?)8.

In 1911 shown as son of a watchmaker, Mr. Walter H., and Maria Pollard of 31 West Buildings, Worthing. He was then a 9 year old boy, born in Worthing in 1892.

A(rthur Henry) Powell Number 17969, Enlisted in Hastings. Private, 7th Bn., Royal Sussex Regiment, died of wounds, 03.05.18, aged 25.

Buried in Etaples Military Cemetery, Grave LXV. A. 29. (? Possibly). Son of James F. and Lavinia Powell of 4 Balvernie Grove, Merton Road, Wandsworth, London. (Listed as 'Native of Wandsworth').

In 1911 this Powell was an eighteen year old Messenger for the Pall Mall Gazette.

There are three possibilities for the last name on the memorial,

V Scott   Number 46971, Gunner, B. Bty., 103rd Brigade., Royal Field Artillery, died 22.11.16.   Buried in Caterpillar Valley Cemetery, Longueval, VIII A.15.

V Scott   Number 260309, Private, Duke of Cornwall's Light Infantry, died 23.08.18. Buried in Queen's Cemetery, Bucquoy. Grave IV. A. 16.

V (W) Scott (MC)   Lieutenant, Royal Flying Corps and 13th Bn., East Surrey Regiment, died 16.03.18.   Buried in Cabaret-Rouge British Cemetery, Souchez.

In 1901, a Victor, born 1897 in London, was living with his family at 39 Edward Street, Brighton. Father Grant Scott, a Licensed Victualler.

In 1911, a Vincent Thomas, aged 16, born 1895 in Sunbury, a Butchers Apprentice was living with parents John Henry and Annie at 19 St. Matthews Road, Worthing.   Father was an Insurance Broker. (Most likely choice).

No V.E. Scott's on 1901 Census in Sussex. A Victor E was aged 4 living with parents, Albert E and Minnie E at 53 Stoke Road, Guildford, Stoke Within. Father was a Boiler Maker. Victor was born in Guildford.

In 1911, a Victor Edward Scott was a 14 year old schoolboy. His father was Albert Edward, a 41 year old Engineer Smith, and mother Minnie Ellen were living at 60 East Ham Road, Littlehampton.

In 1901, a Victor (W) and his family were boarding at 5 Braybrook Terrace, Hastings. His father, Charles W, born in Kilburn in 1866 was a builder. Mother was Matilda C. He was aged 4, and born in Hornsey, Middlesex.

In 1911, his father Charles Walter and mother, Matilda Charlotte were living at Ashmounts, Woodside Avenue, North Finchley, London. He was a Builder and Contractor. No Victor shown. (Possible, less likely).

The named persons who appear to have no connection with Worthing, may have earlier been members of parish families who had left the town and lived elsewhere.

Where there is no certainty for a combatant, the possibilities are noted.

CHAPTER 13

The Final Purdon Years 1915 - 1923

On July 15 1917, Bishop Amigo made his fourth canonical visitation and administered the Sacrament of Confirmation.

Later, on September 4 1917 Fr. Purdon was made an Honorary Canon of the Diocese of Southwark. About this time the outside of the church and the whole of the Presbytery were put in thorough repair.

Canon J Purdon

The Journal informs that on May 3 1918 a memorial Crucifix was placed in the ground of the Church, the gift of Mr. Julian Gaisford - St. Lawrence, and his brothers and sisters in memory of Lt. Col. Walter Thomas Gaisforth, Seaforth Highlanders, Killed in Action Sept 25 1915. R.I.P. On August 4 Pope Benedict granted an indulgence of 100 days to all who recite one Our Father and one Hail Mary before this crucifix. (Earning an indulgence was a means of lessening the time spent, after death, in waiting to enter the Kingdom of Heaven).

On August 1 1918, after nearly ten years service in Worthing as Chaplain to St. Mary's Home and assistant priest to the Mission, Fr.

John Fichter left the Worthing Mission to become a Chaplain to His Majesty's Forces.

Eleven days later, Fr. J. C. Redding entered on his duties as Curate, taking certain duties at St. Mary's Home on Sundays and Days of Obligation and confession on eves of those days; also Benediction. Conditions: Mass once a week on Sunday and Days of Obligation and Benediction on those days. St. Mary's Home would pay a stipend of £30 per annum paid in (advance ? *missing).*

On June 4 1919, the Bishop made his canonical visitation and gave Confirmation.

The congregation at St. Mary's gradually grew, and as a result in 1920 the school was enlarged to accommodate the increasing number of children.

On November 9 1920, Canon Purdon must have been very displeased as he noted ... 'after Mrs. Alderman Chapman was elected first female Catholic Mayor of Worthing: ... dis-edification and scandal, surprises, were caused by her going to the Protestant church in Broadwater and at choosing as chaplain the most bigoted and ignorant rector of Broadwater'.

On January 2 1921 a large stone cross on the last gable was blown down.

Canon Purdon was advised on April 11 1921 'that the school premises were condemned as inadequate in every way. After long correspondence, the Education Department consented as a 'temporary' arrangement of an Army Hut being added and enlargement of playground, new offices and various other details including the loss of the Presbytery garden at the cost of (blank) and the installation of Electric light. All these arrangements were made with approbation of the Bishop and school committee. A most successful Bazaar under the sole direction of Rev. E. J. Redding was held on August 17, 18, and 20 with the object of paying off the debt on the above arrangement, the residue to go to a Fund for the purpose of purchasing land and site for a New School. In 18 hours the sum of £631 was raised at the bazaar; passing 'at once' the whole expense of the temporary extensions of the school premises. A Fund was started for buying the other site which will cost.(Blank)'.

On June 19 1921, the Bishop made his canonical visitation and gave Confirmation and visited the new arrangement and approved of all that had so far been done.

On October 1 1921, a new Cross was placed. The cost amounting to £53.10/-. Messrs. Tate were paid £31.10/- (£31.50) and Messrs. Cheal £22, partly paid by subscription £8.15/-, (£8.75) the rest paid by Fr. Burn.

On October 30 1921 the War Memorial tablet (on East Wall) was unveiled by the Mayor.

On November 9 1921 the Catholic Mayor was re-elected. She came to St. Mary's church this time 'in state' on Sunday Nov. 13. Had Canon Purdon had words with her in the preceding year? It is not mentioned in the papers held in the Archives.

In April 1922 , Fr. E. J. Redding was succeeded by Rev. James Walters. On May 14 of that year, a 'pleasing ceremony' was held to thank Fr. Redding for his work for the parish while he was at Worthing.

Electric light was installed in the church in time for Christmas celebrations of 1922.

In August 1923 a repeat Bazaar was held. It is not known whether it was as successful as Fr. Redding's had been in 1921!

At this time Sunday Mass attendance was estimated to be 600 souls an increase of over 350% since Canon Purdon was appointed to St. Mary's church.

On October 20 1923, Canon Purdon died. He had given fifty-three years of his priestly life to the parish of Worthing and was given a Solemn Requiem Mass attended by the Bishop, many clergy and local dignitaries.

He had asked to be buried in Broadwater Cemetery among his own people. And so he was.

His small gravestone can be found over Grave 2, Row 7 in Block A6.

COLOUR PLATES

St. Mary of the Angels Church, Worthing

Young Thomas Gaisford

Lady Emily, died 1868

Original re-positioned stained glass windows in West wall

1873 Blessed Sacrament Altar - Post 1980's re-ordering

Thomas Gaisford, J.P., died 1898

Memorial to Thomas and Lady Emily on wall above and to the south of the Gaisford internment vault

1902 Holy Souls Altar including, repositioned Statue of Virgin Mary

Memorial Plaque to Canon James Purdon

The wording asks 'In your prayers remember James Purdon Hon. Canon of Southwark, First Parish Priest of this Church, at whose chief cost this altar was erected'.

View towards the West showing 1980's re-ordering

Detail of Corona commissioned in 1980's re-ordering

View of Main Altar from North Transept

The Cross of Christ Choral Evening - March 2015.

Easter Vigil Mass April 2015 – Fr. Benyon celebrating

Mgr. Iggleden

Fr. Rory Kelly

Fr. Tony Shelley

Canon Tony Clarke

Fr. Kieran Gardiner

Fr. Chris Benyon

Parish Priests of St. Mary's from 1966 until date of History

CHAPTER 14

Father Charles Westlake 1923 – 1958

Canon C M Westlake

On November 27 1923, Fr. Charles Westlake came to Worthing. He had held several senior positions in the Diocese including teaching and training students for the priesthood. He had been a Junior Professor in the Seminary at Wonersh, Private Secretary to the Bishop and finally Vice Rector of the Seminary.

In 1924 Fr. James Walters left Worthing to be replaced by Fr. Francis Dorman. In this year the Guild of the Blessed Sacrament held its first meeting on Sunday evening, November 9. Dr. Butcher was elected first Warden. A month later on December 7, twenty-nine men were received into the Guild. Two men were already members of another branch and these thirty one men were the first members of the Guild in Worthing.

Notes in the archives inform of the following items.

On June 22, the Sunday within the Octave of Corpus Christi, a procession of the Blessed Sacrament was held. It commenced in the church and travelled round the street and then entered the convent grounds. It was the first outdoor procession in Worthing. More than 500 people walked in the procession and there were many onlookers.

In August 1924 The Sisters of Our Lady of Sion convent ceased providing the choir for the church services. It was felt that the parish owed the community a deep debt of gratitude for their loyal help during so many years.

A silver gilt ciborium with jewels round the base was acquired by the subscriptions of a few of the congregation. It was used for the first time on Sunday December 7 1924.

A beautiful cope, with Our Lady worked in the hood, was given to the church with a veil, (?) and stole. The set was worked by a sister of St. Mary's Priory, Princethorpe, Rugby and cost seventy pounds. The cope was worn for the first time at Benediction on Christmas Day, 1924.

Fr. Dorman was moved in 1925 to be replaced by Fr. Cecil H. Tasker.

A stone pillar with water stoop attached was under the centre of the main beam supporting the organ gallery. In January 1925 it was taken down and moved a few feet to the south. A second stone pillar was added so as to make a central passage possible up the church.

In February 1926 a Thomas Dyer-Edwardes died suddenly of heart failure in Naples, Italy. He was 78 years of age and had been on a visit to Rome where he was privileged to have an audience with the Holy Father, Pope Pius XI. He had previously been the High Sheriff of Gloucestershire and a J.P. with Thomas Gaisford. He had lived for nine years in 'Charman Dean' and had been a strong Anglo-Catholic. About a year before his death he embraced the Roman Catholic faith and worshipped at St. Mary's. He had presented the church of Our Lady of the Angels (sic) with a new organ. A daughter was a 'Titanic' survivor.

He had been actively interested in the establishment of the Dolling Memorial Home, which became St. Agatha's Home for Girls, at 83 High Street, Worthing. Fr. Robert William Dolling was an Anglican priest doing much to mitigate the evils of slum life in East London. He was continually at loggerheads with the church authorities as a result of his socialistic views. The Dolling Memorial Home had been part of the 'Waifs and Strays' Society. As a training school for twelve girls between the ages of 8 and 14, the home provided an opportunity for learning some valuable skills in housework and laundry. The girls were also taught needlework so they could make and repair their own clothes.

Most of the girls used their training to pursue careers in domestic service.

In 1926 Fr. Westlake was appointed Rural Dean of Arundel and in 1931 he became an Honorary Canon of the Diocese. This must have given him renewed energy for he quickly encouraged the parish to accept greater ideas.

Canon Westlake had a wonderful way of encouraging people to work together and he soon had the people of the parish agreeing that the school facilities in the area west of the church (now the car park) were inadequate. They consisted of the hut that served as the School Hall and two further rooms.

In 1927 the workforce at St. Mary's doubled when both Frs. Thomas Byrne and Maurice Byron joined the team but they were only at Worthing for one year. In 1928 they were replaced by a single priest, Fr. Andrew Shaw.

Adequate education facilities were needed desperately, a Parish Centre was required, and, with the rapid expansion of the town, the church as it stood could not keep pace with the related increase in Mass attendance. The church itself needed to be expanded as well. All these factors would require a large amount of money to be raised, and spent, despite there being, what were believed to be, insurmountable financial difficulties involved.

Lady Winifrede Elwes opening a Garden Fete, August 1927

The ladies enjoying themselves at the 1927 Garden Fete

There appears quite a disproportional number of ladies in these photographs. There is only one man shown in the lower picture for instance. Was this one, at least, a 'female only' stall maybe?

Canon Westlake used his ever present enthusiasm and appreciation of the patience and generosity of his people to overcome these problems using what would now be termed 'man management skills'.

His plans, and Fr. Purdon's before him, began to be fulfilled when in 1928 he bought land on which to build a school. This duly opened in August 1929 with 240 attending, these being junior and senior students between the ages of seven and fifteen years enjoying for the first time the benefits of a purpose built school with appropriate facilities. The schoolrooms in the church grounds, named St. Joseph's, were retained for the education of the infant children between the ages of five and seven years. The new school was called St. Mary's and the first Headmaster was Mr. Albert E. Joy who also became the choirmaster for the church of St. Mary's. Extensions were added in 1935 to accommodate a rapid increase of entries at which time the present school hall was built.

There was a development of large houses in Park Crescent across the road from the church and the end property, No. 14 Park Crescent, now adjoining the school, and further property in Amelia Road became vacant. A year or two before the start of the 1939/45 war, Canon Westlake purchased these properties with extensive gardens for £5100. No. 14 was used as a parish Centre with a Men's Club. A

Youth Club, meeting in the Hut in the church grounds, was operating in the late 1930's. A Discussion Group, for 18 – 30 year olds, was formed. The members met on Sunday evenings after Benediction in No. 14 where they were given a lounge/sitting room for their own use when they weren't rambling or running Sunday-night parish socials in the School Hall. It is recalled that Canon Westlake was quite a strict man and was a little apprehensive of his young ladies and fellows traipsing around the countryside together. There was also a varied programme of activities including a Jazz band, 'hops', table tennis, billiards and a carpentry class. There was also a 'Wireless Club' run by Fr. Donald Wilkins where members built radios from spare parts. These parts were given by a retired doctor with an interest in the subject who lived near the church. It was the Canon's hope that membership of the Discussion Group would lead to marriages between members and several did take place. At least two of those couples are still attending St. Mary's, whose reminiscences are recorded above.

The 'fasting rules' before receiving Communion were rather severe then, when communicants had to fast from mid-night the night before Mass and communion the next morning. Because of this, Holy Communion was seldom received at later Masses in the morning although it was available. One correspondent remembers fainting at High Mass later in the morning for lack of breakfast when she was a child at St. Mary's. In those days people never dreamt that Saturday and Sunday evening Masses would ever be celebrated. In 1954 one couple, mentioned below, had their Nuptial Mass at 9.00a.m. as the priest celebrating it that morning did not want to fast longer than that!

The purchases and developments undertaken left the church with a huge debt. Canon encouraged the parish to raise fundsin many ways including very successful Summer Fetes and Christmas Bazaars held in the school hall. These raised sums of £500 or more, which, at the time, was considered a large sum of money and indicated a very successful bazaar. The headmaster – and church organist - and his family of wife Josie and three sons were very involved with many others in this work.

In 1930, Fr. Shaw was replaced by Frs. Currie and Barraud.

On September 30 1934, Council 280 of the Knights of St. Columba, a fraternal organisation of Catholic men, was created in Worthing. The Headmaster, Albert Joy, was elected as founder Grand Knight, the term used for Chairman. Under his leadership they provided a ready team of manpower whenever needed by the clergy.

In 1934, Fr. Currie left and was replaced by Fr. Andrew Convey.

In 1938 the arrival of Fr. Joseph Sulliway increased the team to four. Fr. Barraud left in 1939 to be replaced in 1940 by Frs. Dennis Cullen and Donald Wilkins. Fr. Convey left in 1942 and Fr. Cyril D. Hanrahan arrived at St. Mary's to stay just one year leaving in 1943 with Fr. Cullen and only Fr. Michael Dunning replacing them. The team was reduced to three until the arrival of Fr. Philip Wroe in 1945.

The congregation continued to grow and the presbytery at 39 Richmond Road was found to be inadequate for the related increase of clergy required. A larger presbytery was required and the solution was found when 68 Gratwicke Road, to the west of the church buildings, was given to the parish. It was large enough to accommodate the Canon and the three curates now in residence and was quickly adapted to create a presbytery far superior to ageing St. Christopher's.

With all the concerns of the parish on his 'doorstep', Canon was concerned for the spiritual welfare of his parishioners from outside the town centre. In 1926 a Mass centre was started at South Street, Lancing in a room lent by a non-Catholic. In 1927, a Mass centre was started in Durrington in a chapel in a bungalow owned by a Mrs. Berry.

In December 1935, a barn with attached land was bought in Goring to be used after renovation as a Mass centre. The area of land would be sufficient to provide adequate space for a purpose built church.

Later, in East Worthing at the Dolphin Public House, with the agreement of both the owner and the licensee, a hired room became a venue for Mass celebration on Sunday.

Extension of the mother church itself, however, was desperately needed. Plans were drawn up and accepted and work commenced in 1938 to extend the nave westwards into what is now the car park. The church hall was adapted to allow church services to be held midweek within giving greater availability of the church to the contractors.

The High Altar at the west end of the nave was moved and a temporary altar erected against partitioning as seen in the photograph below.

Temporary Altar erected in church 1938-39

The church was closed for weekday worship at some time during this period when work on the existing nave and transepts was undertaken. Weekday Mass was celebrated in the Hall, with Sunday Masses in the church when no builders were on site. The High Altar was repositioned on the new west wall and the ceiling woodwork was repeated on the extension. The barrel vaulting that was included in the 1938 re-ordering was left uncovered in the 1983 alterations and can still be seen above the earlier sanctuary.

St. Mary's church hall 1938 – 39

The wooden building shown in photograph above, was in what is now the car park, and was the church hall. A temporary altar, chairs and a shrine to Our Lady were provided until building work was completed.

Work in progress on replaced Altar and reredos

The 1902 statuary on the old west wall was moved and positioned on the new west wall behind the altar where it remains to this day.

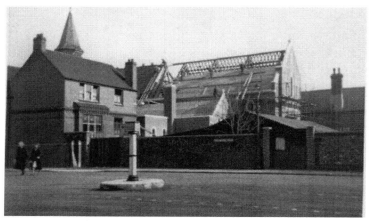

View from Park Crescent of Extension roof work. The Church hall can be seen behind the high wall.

Crucifixion Memorial to Walter Gaisford
Prior to removal in 1938/9

The large crucifix shown above, erected as a memorial to Walter Gaisford, was moved in 1938 and there is no record of its later location. Examining the photograph, the commemorative block in the church courtyard inscribed with his name and details may be the base block of the original as they appear similar in shape.

In 1938 land was acquired at the northern end of Cotswold Road, Salvington. A corrugated iron and asbestos chapel of ease was built for those parishioners in the area of this extremity of the parish.

The opening of the enlarged St. Mary's church took place on July 26 1939. The timing of the building of the extension was very propitious as war was declared so very soon after the completion of the works. Building would not have been allowed during the Second World War.

Ex-parishioner, Marguerite, now in Somerset, recalls confirmation by Archbishop Amigo in 1947 on a very rainy day with the roof leaking very near to where the 'confirmandi' had to kneel in front of the Archbishop.

73

In 1947 Frs. Wilkins and Wroe left Worthing and Frs. Edmund Arbuthnot and Gerald O'Sullivan took their positions. In that year, on 26 July, Circle 133 of the Catenian Association was formed which is an international brotherhood of Catholic business and professional men.

Fr. Arbuthnott was recovering from serious physical injury sustained during the bombing of his presbytery in Dockhead in Bermondsey, London in March 1945. It had been hit by a V2 rocket and totally destroyed. His three fellow priests were all killed and he was presumed dead. He lay in the wreckage for three hours and had an almost miraculous escape. He later wrote in his autobiography that,

'Why I was spared I could not think. I will one day know and I can only assume that unlike the three others I was not ready to die. I must add that throughout those three hours I had a comforting experience of God's protective care. This has largely removed any fears of death that I once had. There was nothing dramatic as far as my part in the episode was concerned'.

He left after a short stay of one year. He retired years later to St. Mary's Home, Worthing as a Canon and the parish were delighted to have his part-time guidance in all things spiritual once again.

His place was filled by Fr. Michael Phelan who was at St. Mary's until 1956 to be replaced by Fr. Richard 'Dickie' Veal. Fr. Phelan had been given charge of the area of Goring until it was given a P.P. of its own in 1952. Fr. O'Sullivan was replaced the following year by Fr. Francis Davys who was joined by Fr. Jeremiah Corcoran in making up once more a full team of four priests.

The school hut, St. Joseph's, with corrugated roof continued to be used as infant school rooms. The roof caused the hut to be boiling hot in the summer and freezing cold in the winter. Two pleasantly remembered sisters taught the children, one was Miss Nevin and the other Mrs. Dear, who was married to a tall policeman, nick-named 'Tiny' Dear.

Realising that new parishes would be needed in the not too distant future, in the early 1950's Canon Westlake had the foresight to buy a plot of land at the corner of Chesswood Road and Ham Road in East Worthing.

Canon Westlake then bought land at Goring in 1953, and this was used for Blessed Robert Southwell School that opened in 1957. St. Mary's school became a primary school including an infants' department filled by those who had previously used the school rooms in the car park. It was unusual then for Catholics to be elected as Town Councillors as was Mr. Farrell, a member of the church who was instrumental in the school receiving a government grant towards the building costs.

Apart from the one mention in the Memoranda by Fr. Whiteside of the opening of the Poor School, with Miss A. O'Brien in charge, there is no further record of the development of this establishment.

The names of the head-teachers of St. Joseph's, apart from Mrs. Dear, are lost in time.

The names of the head-teachers of St. Mary's are:-

Mr. Albert Joy	1929 – 1963	Born 1899; Died 1967
Miss Winifred Wharton	1963 – 1976	Born 1911; Died 1999
Mr. Adrian Bishop	1976 – 1992	Retired 1992
Mr. Gordon Schofield	1992 – 2008	Retired 2008
Mrs. Cecilia Lewis	2008 – to date.	

In 1957 the Worthing Herald published a picture showing that the parish had a thriving Catholic Scout Troop when they were shown passing the Mayor at the Town Hall on a St. George's Day Rally.

In 1958 Fr. Davys moved to be replaced by Fr. Brian O'Sullivan.

All Canon's plans had come to fruition. His beloved children would be given education of a fine level. His young adults had their Youth Centre and St. Christopher's, the old presbytery, had become a Parish Centre.

To add icing to his cake, John Stone and David Patterson, two sons of parishioners, were ordained to the priesthood at St. Mary's, in June 1956, by Archbishop Cyril Cowderoy of Southwark. A photograph of the ceremony is shown overleaf.

Ordination of Fr. John Stone and Fr. David Paterson, June 1956

A very upset and sorrowful Fr. Dickie Veal is remembered having the sad task of coming on to the altar to celebrate Mass and to inform the parish that Canon Westlake had passed away that previous night.

He had died in office on March 1 1958 aged 79 years after serving the parish in Worthing for 35 years. He was buried in Durrington Cemetery on March 6. His Grave is in Section 2, in Row 6 and Plot 57 facing the road on the west side a little way from the main entrance next to the much more prominent grave of ex-headmistress Winifred Wharton that can act as a marker for those visiting the cemetery.

CHAPTER 15
The Second World War and St. Mary's School

During the years when Canon Westlake was parish priest, the world was thrown once more into turmoil when war on a grand scale was again declared with Germany in 1939.

Former pupils, Bert and Vi, remember much below including the large rear garden at 14 Park Crescent being used by teacher Mr. Kinsella for giving gardening lessons to the pupils of St. Mary's school.

The Local Authority commandeered the garden land and Surface Air-Raid shelters were built on it. To help the war effort Victoria Park, close by, was transformed into allotment gardens and the school was given a plot to allow gardening lessons to be continued there.

Albert Ernest Joy had been Headmaster since the school was opened in September 1929. He has been described as having earned the right to join the favoured few who will be remembered as 'characters'. He was a little larger than life, not merely in stature, although he was a big man. He lived his life with gusto and he was the brilliant organist and choir-master at St. Mary's from 1930 until the day before he died.

At the declaration of War in September 1939, the threat of invasion was considered a serious matter. 12,177 children were evacuated from London. Bert Joy had started his teaching career in Peckham, London. Not surprisingly, children from St. Francis R.C. School in Peckham came as evacuees to Worthing and their temporary school was St. Mary's.

Canon Westlake with children evacuated from Peckham, celebrating their first Holy Communion.

They were temporary pupils at St. Mary's school which they shared with the local children on a 'half-day' basis. Soon the scare subsided and the Londoners returned home. A little later the children of Worthing were evacuated from the sea-side town in March 1941 to Mansfield. This was one of the most traumatic matters that affected the parish.

Bert Joy, as he was affectionately called, supervised the move to Mansfield together with Mr. Kinsella and his family, travelling with some parents acting as helpers. The Kinsellas stayed with the children but Bert Joy soon returned to Worthing once the school had settled into their new location.

The children returned home after not too long being away from home as the threat of invasion passed.

The town suffered - but the parish itself was largely unaffected - by the bombing raids on England by the German Luftwaffe. There were several instances of property destruction in the town but the church and convent remained relatively untouched. However, former pupils of St. Mary's remember the school being strafed by a German fighter airplane on February 8 1943. One person received a bullet wound to the arm. A teacher, Mrs. Reid, in a first floor classroom shouted to her pupils to 'duck' and her blackboard was struck by a large fragment of cannon shell. The shattered board fell and knocked her to the floor.

Eight injured children with cuts from shattered glass windows and shrapnel wounds were taken to the Clinic for check-ups and treatment. It was a miracle that nobody had been killed in the attack.

Sadly, there is no method, at the time of writing this history, of discovering the names of parishioners who were killed during the Second World War. The church did not repeat the exercise of providing a war memorial for Second World War casualties from the parish as was done twenty years before. Their names are included on the war memorial near the Town Hall with other casualties from the town.

CHAPTER 16

English Martyrs' Church

The barn bought at Goring was carefully restored and reconstructed to provide a temporary chapel. The alterations were completed in 1937. A Miss Thornly had built a fine presbytery at her own expense for the future resident priest.

The following is a copy of a letter from Canon Westlake which details all that was achieved to lead to the creation of the new parish in Goring,

TO BE READ AT EACH MASS ON SUNDAY, SEPTEMBER 7TH, 1952

During my convalescence in June I approached the Bishop about having a resident priest here and his Lordship has now appointed Fr Desmond McCarthy, who for some years has been the Diocesan Inspector of Schools, to be the first resident priest in Goring since the so-called Reformation. For Goring, then, this is an historic occasion and I know you welcome it.

I bought the land in December 1935 and the reconstruction of the barn into a chapel was finished in time for its opening in 1937, when I had the privilege of saying the first Mass on December 19 and 52 people were present. The War hindered further progress, but since then the number of Catholics has considerably increased and further building will bring a further increase.

At the beginning, of course, Fr McCarthy will have to face financial difficulties; the Offertory for last year came to only £301, and this is the chief source of income. I know you will rally round him and help as generously as possible to make the residence of a priest here permanent; otherwise the only alternative would be to return to the present arrangement of being served from Worthing.

To start with you have this chapel which when the time comes for a church to be built will make a good parish hall; there is also ground for a church. You have also a fine presbytery, the generous gift of Miss Thornly who you should ever remember in your prayers. But the upkeep of this house and the maintenance of the priest is the chief problem. Rates, taxes and insurance have to be met, and the wages of a housekeeper. The house is unfurnished and a certain amount of repair and painting is necessary now – happily I have a certain sum of money in hand to face the latter. But sufficient furniture must be obtained and it would be a great help if some could send me now a donation for this purpose and others offer pieces of furniture, just essential furniture, which they may possess beyond their own requirements. I should be grateful to hear from those who can help in either way. Fr McCarthy hopes to come into residence within a month so time is short.

There is still a debt of £1,400 to be faced. But this is comparatively a small amount of what has been expended here. The total cost of buying the land, reconditioning and adding to the barn, furnishing it as a chapel, came to three thousand and seventy eight pounds; the cost of the presbytery so far as I know cost over three thousand pounds. Of this over six thousand pounds the congregation has been asked to collect only £2,278, owing to gifts from donors outside the district.

I am sure you are grateful for this and for the service of the many priests who have served the chapel and district, and especially Fr Phelan who has been so efficient and so kind since he was given charge of this district. You have given a ready response to all the efforts of the priests who have served you and I feel sure you will welcome and help in every way your first resident priest.

I feel I cannot finish these notes without paying a tribute to the loyal and unselfish service of those who have helped in looking after the chapel or helped on the Sundays – I must not mention names but some have given their service ever since the chapel opened. I feel sure also that they will willingly continue to do so under the new arrangement.

As I cannot come myself to speak to you today I am having these lines read out to you at each Mass today. My curates and myself will miss serving you and will pray that under God the change may be to your spiritual progress.

Charles M Westlake.

Thus the second Catholic church in Worthing became a reality.

The modern English Martyr's church was built in 1968.

CHAPTER 17

Monsignor Denis Wall 1958 - 1966

Denis Patrick Wall was born on 23 December 1918 in Worcester. Denis Wall was ordained on 3 June 1944 after completing his training at Wonersh. He was Chancellor of the Diocese from 1952 until 1958. He was parish priest of Ashford from 1955 before coming to Worthing in 1958 as Monsignor Wall.

Mgr. Denis Wall

His clergy team remained together as both new parish priest and curate took up the task of helping a parish overcome the sadness of losing a priest who many would have known as their only spiritual leader for so many years. It is interesting to note the two previous parish priests had served their flock in Worthing for a total of 88 years, a tremendous achievement.

Monsignor Wall was aware that the income of the parish had to be increased. The growing number of parishioners now living outside the old town limits called for an improvement from Mass centres to churches. A new Senior School was desperately needed.

Ex-parishioner, Marguerite, remembers the seemingly endless years of hearing about the weekly retiring collection for the 'School Building Fund' and the words still ring in her ears.

But something more than collections during the Masses was needed.

The venue for the Christmas Fayre was changed from St. Mary's school hall to Worthing's Assembly Rooms next to the Town Hall. The Fayres had a specific theme each year. It is remembered that one year the theme was 'Holland' when a water-filled canal was formed on which paddled real live ducks. The Fayres were a great success and looked forward to by the whole town in general.

Monsignor also adopted the new idea of running a fund raising activity based on the results of national football games played each Saturday and reported in that days evening paper. He asked the Knights of St. Columba to provide the necessary man-power to run it. The project required a small team of helpers forming a core team, mainly KSC members, receiving monies and producing results and an extensive group of parishioners acting as promoters and selling the necessary membership cards. The cards provided the information to the participants to possibly win a substantial amount of money based on the number of goals that teams in the Football Divisions scored each week.

By law the amount of prize money paid out was fifty percent of the income generated each week. Because the project was very popular – and was adopted by many parishes throughout the country as a serious money provider – considerable amounts of income were generated by this means. In Worthing, the usage of this income cleared the debt incurred on the building and improvement of the schools and resulted in the parish having a healthy bank account to be used for more major projects.

The Parish Priest was very thankful to the fund raising team and their network of agents and this was shown each year when he invited them all to join him for dinner at a local dining venue. One year as an innovation Monsignor took all the workers on a boat trip on the River Thames. It must have been a very successful fund raising year! It has been reported that Monsignor's father was a wealthy man involved in the 'oil industry' and it was the father who financed these memorable occasions.

A new senior school opened in 1957. It was at first called St. Mary's until 1959 when it became the Blessed Robert Southwell Catholic Secondary Modern School. After the canonisation of the 40 English

Martyrs there was already a St. Robert Southwell school in Horsham. Due in some respect to pressure from the Local Education Authority, in 1973 after enlargement, its name was changed to Chatsmore Catholic High School (Comprehensive).

The first change of curate under Monsignor Wall occurred in 1963 when Fr. O'Sullivan moved and was replaced by Fr. Matthew McInerney.

The expansion of the town continued to increase with more and more of its extensive areas of former nurseries being covered by housing estates. Monsignor decided that it was time to use the accumulated funds from what was affectionately called 'the football swindle' to build permanent churches for the growing communities on the borders of the town limits.

Bert Joy led the school for 34 years retiring in 1963. In May 1964 he was awarded the 'Bene Merenti' medal for long service to the church.

In 1964, the Centenary Year of the church, Sunday Mass attendance at the Catholic churches in the Worthing Town area had increased to about 5000 souls.

The stories of St. Charles' and St. Michael's follow in later chapters but it was due to the guidance of Monsignor and the considerable fund raising efforts of the people of St. Mary's that made the new parishes realities - one church cruciform in shape and the other square.

Marguerite remembers also that her family had a French priest as a temporary guest each year. He had to show his credentials to Canon Westlake before he was allowed to say Mass. On one occasion the Canon said 'Don't bother me now, the Bishop is coming' which for some reason struck her as amusing. She also remembers the long queues of people from, the now seldom used Main Doors, round into Gratwicke Road waiting to enter church at Christmas Midnight Masses.

In 1964 considerable changes were undertaken in the church. The ornate pillars were covered or removed and the ornate rood screen taken down.

Several parishioners have expressed the sorrow felt when this work was carried out. It did cause an interesting happening however.

Two parishioners, Roz and Michael, had booked their wedding on a Saturday in September 1964 and all invitations etc, were sent.

Monsignor Wall placed the contracts for the work of the modifications to the church, which was undertaken on a six-day week basis, without considering the bookings for future events. Their Nuptial Mass could not be said in St. Mary's but they were extremely relieved when once more the relationship between Convent and Church was shown to be so strong. Reverend Mother offered the convent chapel for the Nuptial Mass, but a problem was evident when it was realised that the chapel was not licensed for weddings but St. Mary's was.

The outcome was that the workers temporarily ceased work for the time it took for the wedding vows to be made at the altar of St. Mary's. The Register was signed in the room now used as the Repository. Groom, best man and Monsignor hurried through the small doorway in the south east wall of the church into the convent with the bride and her father sedately following behind to complete their marriage with Nuptial Mass in the chapel.

During his final year Monsignor accepted an invitation for St. Mary's to join the Worthing Council of Churches and the parish has been an active member ever since.

With the formation of the Diocese of Arundel and Brighton, Worthing became a parish under the Right Reverend Bishop David Cashman. He had been an Auxiliary Bishop in the Archdiocese of Westminster. The Bishop's Secretary and Chancellor of the new diocese was Fr. Michael Bowen. Fr. Michael had been in the Irish Guards and the Wine Trade before being ordained in 1958. He was ordained Bishop and the Coadjutor of A. & B. on June 27 1970 with right of succession.

Denis Wall had studied at the seminary with David Cashman and from the earliest contact he had had a clash of personalities with his fellow seminarian who was now his Bishop. He asked to be translated back to Southwark in June 1966 when his request was granted.

The parish was saddened at his decision to move away from Worthing. He had been a well liked priest, working continually for the spiritual and physical well being of his people.

He was given the parish of St. Bede's in Clapham Park. In 1967 he moved to St. Francis' in Maidstone, Kent. In 1976 he was given a parish in Westerham, Kent and in 1981 he moved to Barnes in South London. He retired in 1988, dying in October 1992 in Bromley, Kent.

CHAPTER 18
St. Charles Borromeo Church

Monsignor Wall was given outline planning permission in 1958 to use the land bought by Canon Westlake a few years earlier for a church and presbytery. Until the church was ready for use, with the agreement of the owner and licensee of the Dolphin public house in Dominion Road, the Saloon Bar of the premises was used as a Mass centre for the next three years.

In 1959 Bishop Cowderoy of Southwark approved the plans drawn up by Mr. Bingham Towner for a new church to be built on the Chesswood Road site. The church is striking in being in a simple cruciform shape and has a very high ceiling. Church archives show the amount of detailed attention Monsignor gave to the building programme. The total cost of the church was £35,329.

The Catholic Church of St. Charles' was officially registered in April 1962 as a place of worship, the first service taking place in the church in May. A carved and gilded dolphin was positioned by the main entrance to remind the parishioners of the former use of the Dolphin Pub. The family atmosphere of the 'Dolphin Masses' is remembered still.

The next month, June 1962, saw the first baptism celebrated in St. Charles' – and also its first funeral. The first wedding followed in November of that year. Priests from St. Mary's performed these functions.

In January 1963 Father J Colman Quinn was inducted as the first parish priest and St. Mary's parish lost that part of Worthing east of a line consisting of South Street, Chapel Road and Broadwater Road then up Forest Road to the Upper Brighton Road. The eastern boundary was Western Road bordering Brooklands Park with its lake.

The church was dedicated by chief con-celebrant, Bishop Cormac Murphy-O'Connor on June 13 1979.

CHAPTER 19

Monsignor Canon Arthur Iggleden, V. G. 1966 - 1981

In 1966 St. Mary's was placed into the capable hands of the Vicar General of the diocese when Monsignor Canon Arthur Iggleden arrived from his former post as Rector of the Seminary.

Fr. Arthur Iggleden on Ordination Day

In the same year Fr. Corcoran was replaced by Fr. William Dunne.

Monsignor Iggleden was inducted as the parish priest the following year. He was already the Vicar General of the Diocese and was soon exercising his administrative skills in running both St. Mary's and what was, until its formal change to a parish in its own right in 1979, the mini-parish of St. Michaels.

On Easter Sunday, 1967, Albert Joy played the organ at the 11.15 a.m. sung Mass as usual. Soon after returning home from church, he collapsed and died early on Monday morning.

St. Mary's parish lost the third of her beloved and long serving personalities. Canons Purdon and Westlake and Albert Joy had given a joint total of one hundred and eighteen years of service to the church.

In 1967, the newly ordained Fr. Patrick Olivier replaced Fr. Dickie Veal.

Fr. Dunne moved from St. Mary's in 1971.

In that year on March 14 1971, Bishop David Cashman died and Bishop Michael Bowen became sole Bishop of A & B.

The year 1972 saw the arrival of Fr. David Foley and another newly ordained young priest came to Worthing to learn the ropes of priestly life when, straight from Wonersh, arrived Fr. John Nuttall. It was noted that Fr. David was adept in balancing a hand broom on his chin!

Three years of priestly stability followed before Fr. McInerney left St. Mary's, Worthing and was appointed to St. Mary's, Preston Park, Brighton. He was superseded by Fr. Oliver Heaney in January 1975.

One thing that stands out in Fr. Heaney's memory of this time were the huge Christmas Bazaars held in the Our Lady of Sion Convent school halls next door. He was asked to organise them and he was overwhelmed by the scale of the operation under the able leadership of Brian Hodson. The bazaars raised thousands of pounds for the parish and many thought they were the biggest event of the year in both the parish and the town. Vast crowds went along to find a bargain on the many different stalls.

There were always two 'Tombolas' run at the bazaar. The front of the stage in the main hall was used by members of the K.S.C. for displaying a famous, well-provided 'Bottle' tombola with an extensive array including many large bottles of spirits. The parishioners from the St. Michael's area staged a smaller 'General' tombola in the second smaller hall.

The Bazaars provided the bulk of the fund raising income each year. They involved considerable effort on the part of the parishioners but pulled the parish together in a great act of working as a team.

Fr. Heaney recalled that the holding of Christmas Bazaars went back to the time of Monsignor Wall and this was confirmed in written memories produced for this history by people who were parishioners at that time.

Monsignor Iggleden was aware that his parish consisted of the parish church of St. Mary's and also the parish 'in the making' of St. Michael's in the north of the town. He was very fair at this time and had encouraged the congregation in the formation of an efficient Parish Committee. It had a balanced membership both male and female and also in numbers from St. Mary's and St. Michael's. St. Mary's having a Mass attendance much greater than St. Michael's, had the greater proportion of Councillors. The smaller community were very pleased to have a say in the running of the combined parish and to be able to raise matters that only affected their part of the parish. It was apparent that Monsignor always gave a fair hearing to any problems raised that could be overcome. This became very true when he agreed to put their request to the Bishop for the independence of St. Michael's when he considered the time was right for the idea to be viable.

The sacristan at St. Mary's at this time and for many years previously was a delightful little 'old' lady known simply as 'Miss Rule' but there was nothing 'mis-ruled' about the way she so efficiently and quietly did her job for the church, the priests and the parishioners of St. Mary's. She was regarded with great awe because she was allowed to go onto the altar to work on the candlesticks. At the time, women were only allowed on the altar on the day of their wedding.

Pauline Rule retired from her post in February 1990 and this was filled by John Potter until he retired. Arthur Andrews followed John and continued the good work of his predecessors.

The role of Sacristan in any church is a very important one and can easily be unnoticed by many who attend the services each day. St. Mary's has been blessed throughout the years by dedicated people giving great service to the church.

In Autumn 1976 parishioner Kenneth Leach was ordained as Deacon and, although officially appointed to Worthing Deanery on October 4 of that year, served at St. Mary's until his death in 1980.

On April 23 1977 Bishop Michael was translated to Southwark as Archbishop. In the period of the 'inter regnum' between bishops, Mgr. Iggleden was appointed Apostolic Administrator to run the diocese until the new bishop was installed. Fr. Heaney recalls it was a difficult time for Monsignor but he was up to the challenge and enjoyed himself travelling around the diocese in the role of 'Acting Bishop'.

In 1977 Fr. Michael Jackson, another newly ordained priest arrived staying just two years before returning to the seminary to lecture to the students on Theology. He had in the meantime broken his ankle while being encouraged by the altar servers to skateboard for the first time ever around the forecourt of the church and falling off immediately on losing his balance! He remembers hearing a cracking noise but didn't realise the extent of the damage until later in the morning when he tried to genuflect during Mass.

The new Bishop of Arundel and Brighton, Rt. Rev. Cormac Murphy-O'Connor was ordained Bishop on December 21 1977. He arrived in A & B after serving as the Rector of the Venerable English College, Rome since 1971. He began his priestly life in Portsmouth Diocese in 1956.

In 1978 Fr. Oliver Heaney left to become parish priest of Mayfield. That year, the previously unheard of happened. Monsignor Iggleden was elected President of the Worthing Council of Churches. This was a true indication of the improvement in inter-church relationships and the growth of the Ecumenical movement in the town.

In 1979, the vacant position in the number of clergy was filled by Fr. Martin Thompson - again a new priest straight from the seminary.

Fr. Foley was replaced in 1980 by an older priest, Fr. James Maguire.

Father Francis Xavier (F.X.) O'Sullivan was a delightful S.J. priest and member of the staff at the Jesuit Belvedere College in Dublin. In the 70's and 80's he spent his annual summer holiday in Worthing helping with various spiritual tasks in the parish. He was a delightful, very popular and well loved part-time addition to the clergy each year. An important event for Fr. F.X. was his daily morning swim in the sea making the most of his holiday, in particular the long hot summer of 1976 that saw record temperatures – ideal for being on the beach.

As the years progressed, Monsignor Iggleden found the situation of being both Vicar General of Arundel & Brighton and parish priest of a large parish very tiring. In 1981 he decided that it was time to pass the parish over to a younger priest. He retired and became the chaplain to the Augustine Sisters in Kemp Town, Brighton.

He died in Brighton on June 24 2001.

CHAPTER 20

St. Michael of the Angels Church

The history of St. Mary's as a 'Mother Church' and provider for her family was completed by the building and finally the joyful addition to the Diocese of a new parish.

As has been mentioned, areas of the original parish of St. Mary's, - that had been served by Mass-centres had all been upgraded to parishes but for one – the area to the north of the town covering Durrington, Salvington and Findon. In that part of town, from November 1927 a chapel in a bungalow owned by a Mrs. Berry, had first been the venue for Mass. Some time later a 'dingy' corrugated iron and asbestos, mission-style, chapel-of-ease was used as a Mass centre. This had been erected on a piece of land at the north eastern end of Cotswold Road, Durrington, bought by Fr. Westlake in 1938.

The Mass attendance of residents in that area had been slowly increasing and it became obvious that the chapel wasn't large enough for the local Catholic community. St. Mary's had another task to perform – the buying of a larger site and the building of a third daughter church was required.

The parish was very fortunate to be given a house and land in Hayling Rise, High Salvington, by a Mrs. Hughes who was a parishioner, and some finance came from the sale of the land on which the chapel stood. Plans were drawn up with building commencing in early 1965. The following extract from a local paper described the result.

The Worthing Herald, of Friday April 8 1966, featured an article including these words,

'The church (St. Michael's) which has cost £60,000 and taken a year to build was designed by Jones and Kelly, of Dublin.

Sited on the hill overlooking Worthing to the sea, it is of modern design, squarely built. Its interior is a contemporary work of art. The accent is on light, which is amply provided through beautifully-angular stained-glass windows, designed and manufactured by the Irish State Glass Co. of Dublin. The windows are sited so that on a sunny morning a multitude of coloured beams of sunlight shower on the altar.

The outstanding features of the interior are the works of art which adorn it. The 14 Stations of the Cross have been especially painted by

David O'Connell of Chichester, (who died in 1976), and are probably the most revolutionary of their type in any Catholic church in the country. They are certainly the most realistic, bringing the most-narrated story of Christianity completely to life, yet keeping the beauty of facial expression which so many artists have failed to convey. Mr. O'Connell is painting also a picture of the Crucifixion which will go behind the altar. The church at present has accommodation for about 360, but with the addition of more pews and slight re-arrangement it will hold between 800 and 1000'.

The stained glass windows were actually designed by George Stephen Walsh (1911 – 1988) who served his time with the famous Harry Clarke Studios in Dublin.

Mr. O'Connell did complete the huge Crucifixion picture hung behind the altar before his death. Deep study of this picture is very rewarding.

On April 25 1966, the Right Rev. Monsignor David Cashman, Bishop of the new Diocese of Arundel and Brighton performed the Solemn Opening of the church.

St. Michael's continued to be served by the clergy from St. Mary's each priest travelling to Salvington for services on a four-weekly rota.

Mgr. Iggleden was regularly asked to give St. Michael's its independence by the local community. He, in his business like manner, regularly advised them that in his opinion the income from the Mass attendance was not sufficient to successfully support an independent parish.

With the rapid expansion of the north west Worthing area in the 1970's, the Mass attendance grew proportionally. In 1978 Mgr. Iggleden advised the new Bishop that separating St. Michael's from St. Mary's, as a stand-alone parish, was at last a viable idea. Its area would be Durrington, Salvington, High Salvington, Findon Valley, Charmandean and the town north of the Littlehampton Road.

Bishop Cormac formally installed Fr. Harry Salsbury as the first Parish Priest during his Induction Mass on Wednesday July 11 1979.

In 1980, the first year separate records are available, Mass attendance was 312 and 18 baptisms were administered.

St. Mary's was at last a 'stand alone' parish with three local children English Martyrs, St. Charles and St. Michaels around her.

CHAPTER 21

Father Anthony Shelley 1981 - 1990

In 1981 Fr. Tony Shelley arrived at Worthing from the Maryvale Pastoral Centre.

Vatican II guidelines had been produced on the subject of re-ordering of churches to change the layout and improve the liturgical aspect of services. At that time it was also noted that, although there were references in Bishop's Diaries dated 1920 and 1927, St. Mary's had never been consecrated. He felt this anomaly should be remedied.

With the support of Bishop Cormac, Fr. Shelley significantly altered the layout of the interior of St. Mary's church. The very long nave from east wall to west was halved with a centralisation of the altar and church made at the junction of the south and north transepts. An arched Corona with down-lighting was placed above an altar positioned on a raised platform. This gave a much improved visual aspect for all services. Behind the altar, a glass panelled reredos was placed giving a private Altar of Repose in a Blessed Sacrament Chapel in the south Transept. The Baptismal font was positioned to the side of the altar in full view of everyone.

A Grand Auction was among the events organised by the parish to raise funds for these new developments. It was held in the convent car park in Gratwicke Road and was a great success.

Meanwhile, in 1982, Fr. Paul Sankey came to work with Fr. Tony together with a newly ordained seminarian, Fr. Michael Walsh. The parish team was reduced to three priests, an omen of what was to come later, as Fr. Thompson had left the parish to work in Greece in 1981 and was not replaced.

The new-look St. Mary's was blessed and consecrated on Friday November 4 1983 by Bishop Cormac in a grand ceremony attended by the Mayor and his Mayoress and several former Worthing priests.

The changes were considered rather extreme by a small group of parishioners and some transferred their Mass attendance to other local churches. Many of those loyal to St. Mary's remained but found it almost impossible to forgive Father Tony for what they considered a disastrous alteration to the beloved church of their past.

Many have become familiar with the new layout and can see the obvious benefits. More people can obtain a deeper satisfaction from their Mass attendance by being closer to the altar. This is particularly obvious at baptisms and funerals and especially at weddings when the bride and groom are in full view of, and so much closer to, all their family and friends celebrating the event with them.

Fr. Sankey was replaced in 1984 by Fr. Richard Madders who had been ordained in 1978. He was at St. Mary's just a year when he was appointed a Naval Chaplain. He was not replaced leaving the number of clergy as low as it had been 53 years earlier.

Under these circumstances, Fr. Tony split the parish into north and south sections named 'Pastoral Areas' with each priest caring for half of the parish. Each Area would send representatives to the Parish Council. Within each Area, small Faith Sharing Groups were formed. These covered 20 or so roads and all Catholics in an area were encouraged to meet for both spiritual and social activities. House Masses were considered a great success.

This arrangement was found to fade away after Fr. Michael was moved in 1985. He was replaced by Fr. David Sutcliffe, a late vocation priest, filled the role of School Chaplain which he did successfully until 1989.

Fr. Tony renovated the presbytery, the accommodation being brought into line with modern day standards. The ground floor rooms were altered to include a parish office and meeting room.

He also initiated the office of Extraordinary Minister of the Eucharist in the parish. Sick and housebound parishioners benefit in considerable numbers from the actions of these good people.

The number of clergy increased for a year in 1987 when Fr. David Russell joined the parish team but he was soon moved in 1988.

In 1989, Fr. Sutcliffe was replaced by newly ordained Fr. Paul Turner who then became curate to his second parish priest in two years when Fr. Shelley was replaced as parish priest in 1990.

St. Mary's had been blessed with another leader who was always popular with the younger members of the parish. Many groups had spent part of their summer holidays visiting the surfing beaches of Cornwall, or enjoying the waters round Crete, with their friendly parish priest.

CHAPTER 22

Father James Anthony Clarke 1990 - 2004

Fr. James Clarke, known as Fr. Tony, came to Worthing in 1990.

Fr. Paul helped him to settle in and the partnership of experienced parish priest and comparative novice was a great success.

Three years later, Fr. Paul's place was taken by Fr. Anthony Milner yet again a priest newly ordained that year. Was there something special about the parish of St. Mary of the Angels, Worthing that was so beneficial for a newly ordained priest to experience?

During the years 1991 to 1998 Mary Hodson and a team of ladies provided a very welcome service to those older persons in the parish who were living alone, often after being widowed. She organised the preparation and cooking of a Sunday dinner provided during one weekend of each month. The venue was the parish centre, St. Christopher's, and was limited to forty places, these being booked very quickly each month. The smell of roast dinner being cooked often reached into the church during the last Mass on Sunday morning.

Because of dwindling numbers of helpers, the monthly meal became a once a year Christmas dinner from 1996. Due to lack of help these only survived for a few years and lunchtime meals in St. Christopher's ended after Christmas 2006.

In October 1994 Arthur Andrews died. For all his work for Church and community with over sixty visits to Lourdes as a brancardier, his first in 1924 aged 18, he had been awarded the Bene Merenti medal. The post of Sacristan was filled by Anne Challinor who has worked quietly and effectively for the last twenty-one years. With the help of her team of assistants. Anne was herself awarded the Bene Merenti medal in 2006. Fr. Anthony was replaced by Fr. Graeme Thomson in 1996.

In that year, parishioner Robert, 'Bob', Mason became the Rev. Bob Mason on ordination as a Deacon for Worthing Deanery but serving the parish of St. Mary's. He retired from his ministry in 2004 but is always available when needed for special occasions.

In the late 90's Dennis and Jacqueline organised a week-end coach-trip travelling to Morecambe to spend time together with Fr. Tony. It was very successful with everyone, from newly weds to a couple married for sixty years, enjoying each other's company.

Throughout his fourteen years at Worthing, Fr. Tony was found to be a popular and jovial priest who enjoyed socialising with his parishioners.

In 1997 Liz and Steve Longhurst joined the Columban Lay Mission Programme. The parish was hugely supportive of their decision and helped finance them by raising over £1500 for the Columbans. They spent six months on intensive training and were assigned for three years as Lay Missionaries to the Philippines. It was a very enriching, often extremely tough experience, shared with St. Mary's through regular letters. Steve and Liz found the support of the parish an invaluable source of grace and blessing. Very sadly Steve died of cancer three years after their return while they were still working as Columbans with marginalised people in the UK.

St. Mary's last curate was newly ordained Father Paul Wilkinson who had worked in the parish previously as a deacon and returned in 2000 when Fr. Thomson was moved by the Bishop. Having met the parish previously he quickly settled in, at one time having to celebrate Mass, with the admiration of all, on crutches due to suffering an accident.

On March 22 2000, Mgr. Hull, the V.G. of the diocese became Apostolic Administrator when Bishop Cormac was appointed Archbishop of Westminster. The Rt. Rev. Bishop Kieran Conry was ordained as fourth Bishop of Arundel and Brighton on June 9 2001.

The interior of the church was redecorated for the Millenium. High on the northern wall of the north transept of St. Mary's was an elaborate multi-facetted window with plain clear glass. Father Tony Clarke ordered the coloured design that can be seen at the present time.

The glazing of the partition or reredos between the main altar and the south transept also had plain glass. Mrs. Elizabeth Reidy paid for the replacement of this glazing by the coloured design seen at present, in memory of her deceased husband Jack, a very popular parishioner.

About this time Maurice Lingard painted the striking picture, hung below the reredos, of Christ entitled 'King of Eternal Glory'.

Fr. Tony was appointed a Canon by the diocese in 2001 and was given the parish of The Sacred Heart, Cobham, Surrey in 2004. He died suddenly on April 4 2007.

Fr. Paul left to become parish priest of Moulescoomb and Chaplain to Sussex University in 2004.

CHAPTER 23

Father Kieran Gardiner and Father Rory Kelly
2004 - 2007

Fathers Kieran Gardiner and Rory Kelly had worked together as curates in the past and requested of the Bishop that they work together once more. The Bishop duly advised and in 2004 Fr. Kieran became the Parish Priest and Fr. Rory the Administrator of St. Mary of the Angels.

They quickly settled in and soon formed a new parish council under the title of 'The Parish Team'. An innovation was that each of the four Masses had, what was in effect, a Sub-team under its own chairperson called a 'Leaven Group'. A representative from each Leaven Group had a seat on the main parish team. Attendees at each Mass were encouraged to submit ideas or grievances to the representatives of their particular Leaven Group. This system was quite effective with parishioners more inclined to speak and discuss problems with people they knew well as opposed to a member of a more remote Parish Council.

In a similar way to the trip to Morecambe arranged in Fr. Clarke's time, Fr. Kieran arranged a parish holiday to Ireland which was enjoyed by all the travellers. The trip included a visit to the Shrine at Knock.

It was suggested to Fr. Kieran that the parish might benefit from an idea copied from the neighbouring St. Michael's parish. They had formed a Friendship Group of parishioners meeting on a weekday afternoon for social activities. The priests agreed for a similar group of St. Mary's people to meet on a fortnightly basis to begin with and the Worthing St. Mary's Friendship Group began to meet from January 2006.

The new clergy had many ideas to improve the spiritual and social life of the parish but the following example was not the most effective.

For many years it had been realised that the use of the former presbytery was inadequate as a meeting place for any event with an attendance of more than fifty or so. It was decided that the 'Lady Chapel', could be much more effectively used as a social area if the altar and statue were moved to positions elsewhere in the main body of the church.

This change was put into effect in late 2005 when the statue was repositioned below the reredos of the original 'High' altar on the western wall of the main building. A plinth clad with dark wood was placed against the northern wall of the north transept with the statue canopy, or using the correct term the 'tester', from the Lady Chapel being placed there above a statue of the Sacred Heart. The effect was very pleasing to the eye. The original altar in the chapel was temporarily repositioned against the western wall of the area prior to ultimate removal. A statue of Our Lady Queen of Heaven was given to the parish and this was placed on the unused altar that stands in the area opposite the main notice board.

With these changes undertaken the parish at last had an area that could be used for larger gatherings and social activities and it was quickly used as such to the enjoyment of many of the parishioners.

However, the church of St. Mary of the Angels comes under the umbrella of both National and Diocesan Committees as a listed building. Changes to such a building have to be agreed by certain committees before any such proposed changes can be undertaken.

The Historic Churches Committee for the Dioceses of Southwark, Arundel & Brighton, Portsmouth, Plymouth & Clifton had been notified of the changes undertaken in the church. They were very concerned that these works had been undertaken without prior authorisation by the Committee and demanded that the Parish Priest and Administrator submit a retrospective application for these works.

In a document dated March 20 2006 sent after a meeting of the above committee the parish was advised that apart from the repositioning of the Our Lady Queen of Heaven statue, all other work previously undertaken had to be re-instated.

This work was duly undertaken but resulted in the two priests who had care of St. Mary's for a little under four years asking Bishop Kieran for a move to new parishes. These requests were duly agreed and in September 2007 our new parish priest arrived at Worthing from his previous parish in Haslemere.

CHAPTER 24

Father Christopher Benyon 2007 – to date

Due to a slight delay in the new parish priest being available for duties, the parishioners at Worthing needed a supply priest to say Mass. On one particular Sunday evening, a parishioner, who had been asked to prepare the church and altar before Mass, arrived at the church to carry out that duty. He found that the Bishop was acting as the supply priest and in his kind way had completed all the preparation of the church and altar himself. The congregation had the pleasant and unannounced surprise of seeing their Bishop walk onto the altar as celebrant. He addressed the worshippers at each Mass by advising them that he wasn't their new parish priest, only their Bishop.

Fr. 'Chris' Benyon arrived in September 2007 with much experience of leading a parish. His recent parishes had been Merrow with Burpham, 1981 – 1990; St. Thomas More, Seaford, 1990 – 1999; St. Thomas of Canterbury & English Martyrs, St. Leonards, 1999 – 2001 and Our Lady of Lourdes, Haslemere, 2001 – 2007.

He was made Dean soon after arriving.

Through these pages the reader may have observed that there is a certain pattern. There is a cycle of structural change undertaken by one parish priest that is followed by a lack of any such change by the next. And so it has repeated itself with the present incumbent.

But Fr. Chris has not led a life of inactivity but has guided the parish of St. Mary's into a much deeper life of spirituality, worship and caring.

An outline of these activities is included here.

In St. Mary's Parish the church year is considered finished at the end of July, as it is in school-time. The month of August is a time of a reduction in organised activity and Fr. Chris takes his annual holiday at this time.

The start of the New Year is heralded by a Restart Week in early September when the parish organises an in-house Mission with a spiritual exercise after morning Mass and on each evening.

It was suggested that the church could be decorated in keeping with each annual Festival such as Christmas, Easter, and Harvest Thanksgiving for instance. Fr. Chris considered this a great idea and the parishioners have been well pleased with the results produced by the Church Decoration Group, formed to undertake this work.

At dusk, the Bell tower is floodlit and at Christmastide, a Crib Tableau is placed on the flat roof of the repository and also floodlit.

At this time, a Christmas tree placed near the altar is festooned with labels indicating certain items needed as Christmas gifts for those unfortunate people who have little themselves. A label is removed and a corresponding present is placed on the sanctuary and these are distributed accordingly.

Gifts of food and clothing for the Worthing Churches Homeless Project in the town are received in good quantities and passed on for the less fortunate members of our local society.

The Christmas Grand Draw has been revived and provides welcome income each year.

A Liturgy Group was formed to consider and arrange the necessary items needed to celebrate fittingly the various feasts of the year. Arrangements are made concerning music, Special Ministers of the Eucharist, readers, altar servers and many other matters that need to be taken into account for the successful running of a large many cultured congregation. That the services at St. Marys are considered so good by so many of the parishioners, is due in no small part to the diligence of this group, given guidance, where necessary, by Fr. Chris.

One of the most important developments instigated by Fr. Chris has been the installation of a 'web cam' but not for security in the church; that is dealt with by a security camera system. The web cam system was installed in 2010 and is used to supply a visual broadcast of all services at St. Mary's to a worldwide audience. This gives benefits to a range of viewers from the housebound in Worthing unable to attend Mass, to relatives of parishioners from all parts of the world. These people, unable to be present in person, can see, for example, the christening of a new member of their far flung family or maybe the wedding of a distant relative, now living in a new home in our parish.

Strong CAFOD, Justice and Peace and Society of St. Vincent de Paul groups have been encouraged in the parish and the sale of Fairtrade goods is well supported and Worthing's Churches Homeless Organisation is well supported by the parish.

CHAPTER 25
Yesterday Today and Tomorrow

The Easter Season is the beginning of the Church Year. It is the time of the year when the parish benefits most from the endeavours of the several groups involved in the running of the church of St. Mary's. Members of the Church Cleaning Team, Liturgy Group, Choir, Flower Arrangers, church Decoration Team members, Sacristy staff, Altar servers, Readers and Eucharistic Ministers all co-ordinate their efforts and talents. They bring to those great feasts of Easter a tremendous feeling of great spiritual satisfaction. The parish collectively travels into the church rejoicing with palms in hand on Palm Sunday. The humility of Christ is visibly remembered by the washing of feet on Maundy Thursday. The sadness of the Good Friday story, when Christ stands alone in front of Pilate and the congregation denies Him, is carefully and thought provokingly enacted in dramatic form. Then the uplifting ceremony of the Vigil service, enhanced by the use of an audio-visual I.T. presentation, brings the parish to the reality of spiritual life after death for all.

This year, 2015, saw the culmination of seven years of experience. The community of St. Mary's was given what has been considered by many to be the most moving Easter Celebrations they had ever witnessed.

The Decoration and Flower Arranging Teams work very successfully to provide a church full of beauty and meaning for each of the great feasts of the Church's liturgical year.

At daybreak on Mid-summers Day, a Dawn Mass is celebrated on the Downs and attended by a considerable number of people. It is a very moving and spiritual experience when the appearance of the rising sun, behind Fr. Chris, coincides exactly with the act of Elevation of the Host. A shared 'al fresco' cooked breakfast follows.

Harvest Festival is now part of our ritual with the church decorated accordingly and gifts of produce placed on the sanctuary by parishioners to be distributed to the Worthing Homeless Project.

Armistice Day in November is fittingly remembered when a wreath is brought to the altar at each Mass and the National Anthem is sung. A wreath is then placed on the Memorial to the War Dead on the external east wall that lists the names of those lost in the First World War.

The parish priest is extremely keen to give blessings to those who have a particular role in life, such as mother, father or teacher. On their special day, just before the closing prayers of the Mass, parishioners with one of these roles are asked by Fr. Chris to stand and receive a blessing on that particular day.

The parish is invited to attend 'Journey in Faith' evenings when they have the opportunity to deepen their faith. These meetings are open to non-Catholics and have been instrumental in bringing new members into the Catholic Church and our congregation.

A regular event in the monthly calendar of St. Marys is the First Friday Healing Services. These take place after morning Mass and are very well attended. Fr. Chris has the support of two local Deacons to assist him on the laying on of hands.

There are several Prayer Groups meeting on a weekly basis.

Those attending services at St. Mary's are welcomed by members of a team especially employed for that role.

The Worthing St. Mary's Friendship Group has continued to flourish and is considered by some to be the most successful group the parish has had since the days of Guilds and Confraternities. It continues to meet on a fortnightly basis and the numbers registered on the membership list vary from thirty to the low forties.

In July 2013 parishioner Robert, 'Bob', Smytherman was elected Mayor of Worthing for a year. It is believed he became only the second Catholic to hold this position. Alderman Mrs. Chapman was referred to in Chapter 13 as the first female Catholic Mayor. Bob had been a Councillor since 2002 representing Tarring Ward. Fr. Chris was appointed the Mayor's Chaplain. Bob was a 'local' boy with family connections to Worthing for over two hundred years. He attended St. Mary's Primary School. He has recently been the Town Crier.

As so often happens, good news is interspersed with bad. And so with St. Mary's. In recent months there have been found areas of the church buildings that have shown that the church has been standing for a great number of years. Serious and costly repair work is required to retain the church as a place of public worship. Necessary upgrading of toilet facilities to fulfil the requirements of modern life add to the monetary burden imposed on the community at this time but the parish will once again rise to the challenge as it always has done.

The parishioners were delighted to welcome Archbishop Peter Smith of Southwark to be Chief con-celebrant at the celebration marking the 150th anniversary of the opening of St. Mary of the Angels.

The very successful Mass that took place on Tuesday November 4 2014 was with a full church enjoying a deeply spiritual service with music and singing of a high standard. The church was re-dedicated and blessed anew for the work required to be undertaken in the time ahead.

Those years may well be described in a further volume of the history of St. Mary's, Worthing, written later at the bi-centenary of the parish.

The parish is now participating in a period of rejoicing for the completion of the one hundred and fifty years that St. Mary's has served the town of Worthing. Many events are planned from simple prayer meetings to Concerts and Choir recitals. It is hoped that they will all be enjoyed by many.

The present congregation meet within the walls of the Church of St. Mary of the Angels, Worthing, that have been standing for one hundred and fifty years. It is very pleasing to recall all the prayer and praise that has been presented to God in this building by many, many Christians.

This has been possible because of the efforts of those people who so many years ago decided that a Catholic church was needed and then strove to undertake the work required to provide the church in which we worship today.

That effort has been mirrored year by year by a multitude of people who have continued that work for the parish and local community.

Those people come from diverse backgrounds and cultures which has been repeating itself over many decades.

The Irish nation has been the source of many new individuals and families leaving their homeland to find employment in England. A large part of many Catholic communities can trace at least one line of their family tree to Irish ancestors and St. Mary's is no doubt no exception.

After the Second World War between 1945 and 1960 the parish became home to many Italian families who were invited to work in the extensive horticultural businesses for which 'Sunny Worthing' was so well known. This can easily be seen in the following graph.

Falls in the numbers of worshippers can be accounted for in some part in 1963 when St. Charles parish opened with 200+ parishioners and in 1978 with the formation of St. Michael's when 300+ parishioners were transferred from St. Mary's to that parish.

Any further decline in numbers may be attributed to post-Vatican II attitudes for many brought up as Catholics who no longer feel the need to follow the teachings of the Church regarding Sunday Mass attendance.

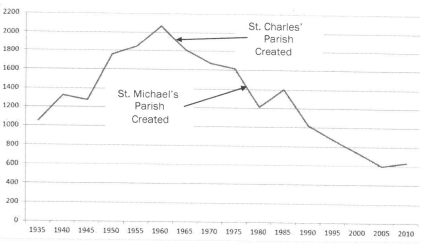

Graph showing Mass Attendance – 1935 – 2010

In recent years the town has welcomed a considerable number of Indian and Filipino people, many of these working in our health services. Many Eastern European people live here now and work in the not now so extensive local horticultural industry. Unlike previous inputs of Irish and Italians when there were only two Catholic churches in Worthing, the influx of these new people is now spread between all four Catholic churches in the town thus explaining a lack of any high spikes on the graph in recent years.

These groups, joining our parish family from far away homelands, have led to an extraordinary event. Each year in March an International Mass brings people together in a joyful celebration in our parish church from twenty three different countries many in National costume.

The Parish of St. Mary's, Worthing is involved in inter-church and international activity supporting both national and international projects, helping those less fortunate members of the present day, materialistic society in which we live. The generosity of our caring church has always been evident in the results of the regular requests that are made to St. Mary's for monetary support for so many worthwhile causes.

If all goes to plan, this current year of 2015 will continue as a memorable anniversary year in more ways than one.

The Diocese will be celebrating its fiftieth anniversary of formation with a Day of Rejoicing and Thanksgiving on July 5 at the Amex stadium in Brighton. A full day is planned and all are encouraged to share this day together when there will be events for every age and church interest organised by the Diocesan Jubilee Team.

On March 22, we were informed that Pope Francis had appointed Rt. Rev. Bishop Richard Moth as the new Bishop of Arundel and Brighton transferring him from his former post as R.C. Bishop to the Forces. He will be presented to the Diocese at the celebration on July 5.

Fr. Chris will be celebrating and thanking God for his Golden Jubilee of Ordination on June 12.

On September 4 the parish will close this anniversary year with a celebratory Mass when we our new Bishop will join our priest and our international parish family in thanking God for all the people and great events and developments that have been recorded in these pages.

Yet another event will be happening when the St. Mary's community experience the greatest of changes at the end of September. After being at Worthing caring for us, for the last eight years, Fr. Chris has advised the parish that, following guidelines by the Hierarchy, he will be retiring as he reaches the age of seventy-five years on September 23. The parish awaits with anticipation the results of the deliberations of our new Bishop on this matter. Those worshipping at St. Mary's fully understand the problems with which the Church is burdened in respect to the decline in clergy but trust they will be given a priest of their own.

Whatever the future holds for the community at Worthing, another new chapter will begin in the life and history of the Parish of St. Mary of the Angels - or maybe Our Lady of the Angels - whichever you believe is the true title.